# NON-NEGOTIABLE

SHEILA LIAUGMINAS

# Non-Negotiable

*Essential Principles of a Just Society and Humane Culture*

IGNATIUS PRESS SAN FRANCISCO

Cover design by Milo Persic


ISBN 978-1-58617-794-2
Library of Congress Control Number 2013909316
Printed in the United States of America ∞

*Dedicated to*
*Fr. Andrew Liaugminas*

# CONTENTS

# PREFACE

We the people are losing our ability to think clearly or reason well. We are largely unable to have civil discourse and have virtually lost the art of argument. We no longer even have a common language with the moral grammar of our Founders, the grammar of ethics that formed the Judeo-Christian tradition which shaped and directed our nation. Religiously informed voices and politically motivated ones are talking past each other, apparently without realizing their mutual source and goal. In other words, the ideals of modern democracy are Christian in origin, and they form the pillars required to hold up a flourishing society.

The characteristically Christian element of our nation is its foundation upon the *inalienable dignity of the human person.* The human person is the pinnacle of God's handiwork. God so loved this human creature that he sent his own Son to become one among its number—and not only that, but to give the ultimate sacrifice for human salvation. That was how much God loved humanity. And not just humanity in a vague, amorphous sense, but each and every human person—especially the smallest, the least, and the forgotten. No matter what state they are in, people have dignity and deserve to be treated accordingly. Period.

Of course, it takes a lot to live this out in practice. Far too easy it is to be like the character Pierrot in Edna St. Vincent Millay's play *Aria da Capo* (1920) and see no incongruity in saying: "I love Humanity; but I hate people!" But it is real flesh and blood people, you and I, who make up humanity. So does the child in the womb, the person in the gutter, and the patient relying upon medical nutrition and hydration for life. When it comes to us humans, certain truths are so foundational for our life and flourishing that they are simply not open to debate or mitigation—they are *non-negotiable.*

# INTRODUCTION

*One of the most important human values is doubtlessly the right to life, to be protected from the moment of conception up to the moment of natural death. However, it must be considered a serious paradox that this right to life is threatened precisely by today's highly advanced technology. Such a paradox has reached the extent of creating a "culture of death", in which abortion, euthanasia, and genetic experiments on human life itself have already obtained or are on the way to obtaining legal recognition. How can we not make a correlation between this culture of death in which the most innocent, defenceless, and critically ill human lives are threatened with death, and terrorist attacks, such as those of 11 September, in which thousands of innocent people were slaughtered? We must say that both of these are built on contempt for human life.*[1]

—Francis Cardinal Arinze

*The propitious smiles of Heaven can never be expected on a nation that disregards the eternal rules of order and right which Heaven itself has ordained.*[2]

—George Washington

Over a year into the American Civil War, President Abraham Lincoln had an epiphany on an issue that had nagged him to that point, something he had tried to reckon with in different ways, but he had been frustrated at each turn. Slavery, he came to realize, was not an issue tied up with other issues in the contentious debate and rhetoric dividing the nation. Slavery was at the heart of the rebellion, and it was a moral issue more than a military or political one. Dedicated to eliminating it

[1] Cardinal Francis Arinze, Pontifical Council for Interreligious Dialogue, "Buddhists and Christians: Promoting a Culture of Life for the Future", Message to Buddhists for the Feast of Vesakh 2002, http://www.vatican.va/roman_curia/pontifical_councils/interelg/documents/rc_pc_interelg_20020409_vesakh2002_en.html.

[2] George Washington, "Inaugural Address", Apr. 30, 1789, *National Archives and Records Administration*, http://www.archives.gov/exhibits/american_originals/inaugtxt.html.

finally, Lincoln delivered the Emancipation Proclamation to his cabinet and pushed past opposition on both sides in order to make emancipation and racial equality a central war effort by the beginning of 1863. Near the end of that year, his Gettysburg Address was dedicated to the equality of all people as a foundational issue for a moral union of states.

But he had to do more before the Civil War ended to eliminate the risk that slavery would be reinstated. Lincoln dedicated himself to securing emancipation once and for all through ratification of the Thirteenth Amendment, abolishing slavery. It was early 1865, and factions of Republicans and Democrats with different political goals justified pushing back on slavery for other issues they each considered more important. For Lincoln, nothing was more important, and this was not something he could not secure. In other words, it was for him not negotiable. In spite of politics, and through dedication to a singular principle of human dignity and equality, he secured just enough votes to get it done.

A few months later, in a meeting with former U.S. Supreme Court Justice John Campbell at the Confederate White House, "Lincoln listed three non-negotiable presidential demands: restoration of federal authority in the South; no retreat from his commitment to former slaves; and unconditional surrender of Confederate troops."[3]

He never wavered in his dedication to the principle of human dignity and equality as the core of a just nation. "Lincoln would never retreat from his pledge to keep slavery contained; indeed, his insistence on the gradual extinction of slavery was a non-negotiable element in his Unionism ..."[4]

* * *

How does a nation, or any large community of peoples, determine what is true, right, and good in structuring its governing documents? To what authority do drafters of those guiding principles refer, and to what end?

The Declaration of Independence appealed to "the Laws of Nature and of Nature's God" in its opening statement, "to assume among the

[3] James F. Simon, *Lincoln and Chief Justice Taney: Slavery, Secession, and the President's War Powers* (New York: Simon & Schuster Paperbacks, 2006), p. 277.

[4] Richard Striner, *Father Abraham: Lincoln's Relentless Struggle to End Slavery* (New York: Oxford University Press, 2006), p. 139.

powers of the earth, the separate and equal station" to which God entitles them. The very next line claims and orders that entitlement: "We hold these truths to be self-evident, that all men are created equal, that they are endowed by their Creator with certain unalienable Rights, that among these are Life, Liberty and the pursuit of Happiness."

The United Nations' *Universal Declaration of Human Rights* was drafted by the Commission on Human Rights, which included the prominent French Catholic philosopher Jacques Maritain. It opens with this Preamble:

> Whereas recognition of the inherent dignity and of the equal and inalienable rights of all members of the human family is the foundation of freedom, justice and peace in the world,
>
> Whereas disregard and contempt for human rights have resulted in barbarous acts which have outraged the conscience of mankind, and the advent of a world in which human beings shall enjoy freedom of speech and belief and freedom from fear and want has been proclaimed as the highest aspiration of the common people, ...
>
> Whereas the peoples of the United Nations have in the Charter reaffirmed their faith in fundamental human rights, in the dignity and worth of the human person and in the equal rights of men and women and have determined to promote social progress and better standards of life in larger freedom,
>
> Whereas Member States have pledged themselves to achieve, in co-operation with the United Nations, the promotion of universal respect for and observance of human rights and fundamental freedoms,
>
> Whereas a common understanding of these rights and freedoms is of the greatest importance for the full realization of this pledge,
>
> Now, Therefore THE GENERAL ASSEMBLY proclaims THIS UNIVERSAL DECLARATION OF HUMAN RIGHTS as a common standard of achievement for all peoples and all nations, to the end that every individual and every organ of society, keeping this Declaration constantly in mind, shall strive by teaching and education to promote respect for these rights and freedoms and by progressive measures, national and international, to secure their universal and effective recognition and observance, both among the peoples of Member States themselves and among the peoples of territories under their jurisdiction.[5]

[5] *The Universal Declaration of Human Rights*, Dec. 10, 1948, http://www.un.org/en/documents/udhr/index.shtml.

Then it begins enumerating these rights:

Article 1.

- All human beings are born free and equal in dignity and rights. They are endowed with reason and conscience and should act towards one another in a spirit of brotherhood.

Article 2.

- Everyone is entitled to all the rights and freedoms set forth in this Declaration, without distinction of any kind, such as race, colour, sex, language, religion, political or other opinion, national or social origin, property, birth or other status.

Article 3.

- Everyone has the right to life, liberty and security of person.[6]

The United States as a nation and the United Nations as a body of global representatives have within them powerful forces passing laws and advancing agenda that totally violates a number of the principles established in both declarations.

How did this happen? How can a ruling class so boldly disregard "self-evident truths" and return to having "disregard and contempt for human rights", ignoring declarations that should ground their every action? How can they have constructed a new set of priorities that violate their founding principles, and advance them under the language of "rights" based on nothing more than shifting cultural relativism?

Most people have never heard of Edmund Gettier, but he's a perfect study for where we are right now with social, cultural, academic, political, and media elites controlling the message about who we are as a society and what constitutes our common good. Gettier presented to the established hierarchy of philosophers of the twentieth century a simple, three-page paper asking the right question: "Is Justified True Belief Knowledge?"[7] He thereby challenged all that they intuitively called knowledge, and he inspired a great deal of work by philosophers attempting to recover a workable definition of knowledge.

We have an establishment hierarchy of culture-shapers today who hold a shared ideology treated as evolved knowledge, and it's based on a

[6] Ibid.

[7] Edmund L. Gettier, "Is Justified True Belief Knowledge?" *Analysis* 23 (1963): 121–23.

secular humanist definition of the "person" that doesn't hold up to the scrutiny of reason. It is mostly an atheistic, agnostic view of the universe relying mostly on science, with no concept of evil, no concept of the spiritual life or an afterlife, and not based on any doctrine but only on evolving cultural trends and experiences. It's a relativistic and utilitarian ideology, mostly shielded from scrutiny by major media who happen to share it. They simply believe it is true and enlightened.

But what's the gauge for truth? Jesus stood before Pontius Pilate and said, "For this I was born, and for this I have come into the world, to bear witness to the truth. Every one who is of the truth hears my voice." But the powerful governor asked, "What is truth?" (Jn 18:37–38). He must have been worried about it, because he kept trying to find a way out of condemning a man in whom he found no fault.

Those who heard Christ's voice then carried on his teachings unchanged throughout history, and Christians are still challenging other truth claims that don't apply the whole Gospel or even make reference to it. Why? Because the profoundly human truths embodied in Christ are, "quite simply, the truth about everything", in the words of the late scholar, theologian, human rights activist, and author Fr. Richard John Neuhaus.[8]

Catholics imbued with the riches of teaching and Tradition should have a penetrating spirituality that pervades their decisions and actions, a devotion to God, to mankind, and to truth. In one of his Wednesday audiences leading up to Pentecost 2013, giving catechesis on the Creed, Pope Francis focused on the actions of the Holy Spirit. "We are living in an age when people are rather sceptical of truth", he said.

> Benedict XVI has frequently spoken of relativism, that is, of the tendency to consider nothing definitive and to think that truth comes from consensus or from something we like.... The truth is not grasped as a thing; the truth is encountered. It is not a possession; it is an encounter with a Person.
>
> St Paul teaches that "no one can say 'Jesus is Lord' except by the Holy Spirit" (1 Cor 12:3).... We need to let ourselves be bathed in the light of the Holy Spirit so that he may lead us into the Truth of God, who is the one Lord of our life.... We are not Christian "part-time", only at certain moments, in certain circumstances, in certain decisions; no one can be

[8] Richard John Neuhaus, *Death on a Friday Afternoon: Meditations on the Last Words of Jesus from the Cross* (New York: Basic Books, 2000), p. xi.

> Christian in this way; we are Christian all the time! Totally! May Christ's truth, which the Holy Spirit teaches us and gives to us, always and totally affect our daily life.[9]

But we don't behave that way often enough. As Pope Benedict XVI also said often, we live in a culture unmoored from its Judeo-Christian roots, an increasingly secular culture with no reference to God. In this environment, he warned, tolerance has degenerated into indifference toward permanent values. But even though Christians are reluctant to make a public witness to faith in this prevailing secular culture, he also warned that resigning ourselves to public indifference to truth was the heart of the crisis of the West. If truth does not exist, Benedict said many times, then mankind cannot distinguish between good and evil.

That seems self-evident. But so did the truths declared by the Founding Fathers. They no longer are.

We have vast means of communication available today for engaging individuals and communities globally. These should invoke our passion, compelling us constantly to seek objective truth and share it with others, as we share so many other thoughts incessantly through social-networking media.

That's very difficult in an increasingly radical secular culture that rejects the transcendent and ridicules claims of truth. At best, it's relative. But as Pope Benedict calmly affirmed, even in a world of fallen-away Catholics and other Christians, the seeds of the future of the world remain in the faithful Church found even in small communities of faith. There are many communities of faith, who understand "Catholic social justice" or even "social justice" in their true sense, before these concepts became redefined by politics. Many of them have practiced it for decades, from years of delivering food and clothing to the poor, or visiting the blind or other disadvantaged people, or bringing relief to the suffering. Human dignity is etched in their consciousness without being a topic to single out for thought or study.

Until it is glaringly violated.

Decades ago, a little girl accompanied her father on his only business trip to the deep South, her first time to leave their Midwestern town.

[9] Pope Francis, General Audience, Wednesday, May 15, 2013, http://www.vatican.va/holy_father/francesco/audiences/2013/documents/papa-francesco_20130515_udienza-generale_en.html.

Besides the new and different and "strange" sights, there was the ominous, the different way people reacted to each other. They were in a drugstore in Alabama, and she saw a fountain with the sign "No Coloreds Allowed", and she was outraged. In the loud voice of an indignant child who doesn't think of or care about the setting or context but only the boiling need to cry out, she shouted, "Dad! They can't do that! They can't treat people that way! *That's not right!*"

That was her initiation into "social activism". She didn't know much about John F. Kennedy but was glad a Catholic was elected president and that he emphasized service. She followed Dr. Martin Luther King, Jr., and admired his peaceful protests and soaring sermons and addresses. And his noble dignity. That impression left an imprint on this little girl's conscience.

True story. That little girl was me.

I continued to work for peace and social justice through the Church and the profession of journalism. I landed in adulthood during a turbulent time when social morals and values, bedrock principles, and Gospel truths about human dignity and equality got contorted out of recognition. Why are we seemingly closer to world war than world peace, after the lessons of the twentieth century should have been so obvious that we could not repeat its mistakes?

Look at some of the events of 1963 as emblematic of the era of human dignity, rights, and freedom.

On April 11, 1963, Pope John XXIII issued his Encyclical *Pacem in Terris* (Peace on Earth), which called attention to the "signs of the times" and built an appealing argument that *peace* will only be a word devoid of meaning unless it is made a cause based on the order "founded on truth, built up on justice, nurtured and animated by charity" and practiced in freedom.

On April 16, 1963, Dr. Martin Luther King would issue his famous and eloquent Letter from Birmingham Jail to fellow clergymen about why he saw the need for the March on Birmingham,

> because injustice is here. Just as the prophets of the eighth century B.C. left their villages and carried their "thus saith the Lord" far beyond the boundaries of their home towns, and just as the Apostle Paul left his village of Tarsus and carried the gospel of Jesus Christ to the far corners of the Greco Roman world, so am I compelled to carry the gospel of freedom beyond my own home town. Like Paul, I must constantly respond

> to the Macedonian call for aid. Moreover, I am cognizant of the interrelatedness of all communities and states.... Injustice anywhere is a threat to justice everywhere.[10]

The civil rights movement was fully engaged that year in activism intended to gain new rights and freedoms for African Americans, and the Kennedy administration averted a clash by announcing in June 1963 the proposal that the civil rights struggle confronted the country "primarily with a moral issue. It is as old as the scriptures and is as clear as the American Constitution."[11]

In August 1963, Dr. Martin Luther King and other civil rights leaders led the March on Washington. There he delivered his famous "I Have a Dream" speech, making reference to Abraham Lincoln's Emancipation Proclamation, the Declaration of Independence, and the U.S. Constitution, which he claimed were still unfulfilled for black Americans.

In November 1963, President John F. Kennedy, Jr., was assassinated, having set civil rights legislation in motion.

And in December 1963, the Second Vatican Council, already fully engaged for a year, issued *Inter Mirifica*, the Decree on the Media of Social Communications. In it, Pope Paul VI and the Council Fathers recognized the power and influence of media and took "a moral outlook" at the use of media. "The first question has to do with 'information,' as it is called, or the search for and reporting of the news", it stated, because "not all knowledge is helpful, but it is charity that edifies."[12]

How far we have strayed from that and other standards of the common good, of recognizing the correlation between individual and legal acts of violence that happen in every abortion, and mass slaughter, as Cardinal Arinze stated in the quotation at the beginning of this introduction. And we fail to see the moral wrongfulness of a freedom, as Lincoln puts it, such as so-called "freedom of choice", so analogous to slavery.

[10] Martin Luther King, Jr., Letter from Birmingham Jail, Apr. 16, 1963, African Studies Center, University of Pennsylvania, http://www.africa.upenn.edu/Articles_Gen/Letter_Birmingham.html, © 1963 Dr. Martin Luther King, Jr., © renewed 1991 Coretta Scott King, reprinted by arrangement with The Heirs to the Estate of Martin Luther King Jr., c/o Writers House as agent for the proprietor New York, N.Y.

[11] David J. Garrow, "Martin Luther King Jr.: The Man, The March, the Dream", *American History Magazine*, Aug. 2003, citing John F. Kennedy, "Report to the American People on Civil Rights", CBS News Special Report, June 11, 1963.

[12] Second Vatican Council, *Inter Mirifica*, Decree on the Media of Social Communications, (Dec. 4, 1963), no. 5.

We are living, as both Pope John Paul II and Pope Benedict XVI have warned, as if God did not exist. The popes and bishops and other religious and moral leaders have warned of history repeating itself and the dangers of an elite class redefining humanity, freedom, rights, and even religion.

In his book *Memory and Identity*, Pope John Paul II likens what happened in Poland after the Marxists came to power with "the philosophical developments that occurred in Western Europe in the wake of the Enlightenment", with its abandonment of Christianity as a source for understanding the human person. "All that remained was the idea of God," he said, "a topic for free exploration by human thought."[13]

Therefore, "the foundations of the 'philosophy of evil' also collapsed." This is a critical point, because as John Paul states, evil "can only exist in relation to good and, in particular, in relation to God, the supreme Good". It was a gravely consequential collapse. "All this, the entire drama of salvation history, had disappeared as far as the Enlightenment was concerned. Man remained alone: alone as creator of his own history and his own civilization; alone as one who decides what is good and what is bad, as one who would exist and operate *etsi Deus non daretur*, even if there were no God."[14]

Competing ideas about what constitutes a good life are capturing the attention of contemporary Catholics alongside other members of modern society. The Church has been less of a reference point since the Council. Just after the election of Pope Benedict, the *Christian Science Monitor* ran an article that represented the general tenor of media coverage of a Church and Pope they handicapped with misperceptions. It suggested that observers "inside and outside the church ... see his election as widening the global religious 'red-blue' divide between conservative moral absolutists and liberals of all faiths who say religion must be more inclusive."[15]

This is how his papacy and the Church were framed.

> Against the dominantly secular and relativist mood in Europe, Benedict seems likely to present a firm Catholic conviction, rooted in a starkly black-and-white view of the world. That view is likely to clash with

[13] Pope John Paul II, *Memory and Identity: Conversations at the Dawn of a Millennium* (New York: Rizzoli, 2005), p. 10.

[14] Ibid.

[15] Peter Ford and Sophie Arie, "Benedict XVI Will Test Religion's 'Red-Blue' Divide", *Christian Science Monitor*, Apr. 21, 2005, http://www.csmonitor.com/2005/0421/p01s03-woeu.html.

> mainstream European thinking over many issues widely regarded here as human rights: birth control, gay unions, women's rights, euthanasia, and stem cell research, all areas where European governments tend more and more to ignore Church teaching.[16]

Since that was written, it has become more and more true of the United States as well. What is our response to each of these challenges? We can take Gettier's approach and prod established opinion makers with rational arguments—the right questions—to provoke thought about matters they hold as prevailing "knowledge" of the common good.

How does the average Christian do that, at a time of such information explosion that the great wealth of teaching about philosophy, theology, the bridge between faith and reason, and anything else that requires a ready answer for hot-button, social moral issues seems so inaccessible to busy people with little time and short attention spans? We need our answers to be reachable, accessible, and easy enough to understand that we can make the argument in the public arena of ideas.

A very resourceful and knowledgeable scholar asked me to recommend a book for a Respect Life group heading into an election and confused by all the arguments they were hearing about the moral issues involved in candidates' and parties' positions. They needed a book on what the Church teaches and why, he said, with some frustration over the fact that people weren't accessing the wealth of Church teaching in longer form.

"Sure, I have that", I told him, and searched my shelves for what I was confident was there, having so many books. But I couldn't locate such a book. The theological scholar had many books too, but he hadn't found it yet either. I realized it needed to be written.

Lay people today are consumers of Internet news, cable news, talk radio, the blogosphere, and social-networking media especially. They get their information in quick sound bites with messages that appeal more to emotion than reason. Papal encyclicals and Church documents are not usually tailored to this kind of access. The average person wants current event–driven information.

Journalists cover a wide swath of news and read longer-form texts and legal documents and encyclicals, trying to find the nuggets in them, the hidden and salient points. Often, it's surprising how common the

[16] Ibid.

threads are running through otherwise disparate stories. That represents what you will read in this book.

Chapter One asks a question of self-examination for us, essentially, "Who are we?" and considers what it means to be a nation of humane people. Chapter Two covers the most basic and fundamentally important question, "When does life begin?" It deals with the crucial topic of abortion. Chapter Three addresses end-of-life issues, especially euthanasia. And yet the fundamental issue is the sanctity of life, and they can't be separated, so the issue of ending youngest human life comes up again in the third chapter along with ending other vulnerable human life, especially since it also covers embryonic stem cell research and cloning. Chapter Four on marriage by necessity considers its importance to children, so the themes continue to merge. Chapter Five covers the fundamental freedom of religion and its guarantee by the nation's Founders. But since that liberty has been threatened by a government mandate to violate conscience and provide access to life-ending drugs, the sanctity of life topic permeates that chapter as well.

The ending is really a beginning, because we're in a pivotal point in history in which we have to make bold choices about what our principles compel us to do to protect and advance what we believe. Complacency is not an option. Being a bleeding heart doesn't mean holding a particular political persuasion, but it does mean making tough decisions about time and talent and resources well spent, at the service of others, according to a moral code and a well-informed conscience. The term *political correctness* is irrelevant because politics don't determine what's correct. Similarly, the term *values voters* is illogical, because everyone holds some set of values, and all voters choose whose values will prevail in government.

This is the beginning of a new era in America, in the Church, and culture, one that calls for the uprising of citizens committed to engaging the culture in the public arena of ideas. That starts with discernment of which ideas are relative and which derive from unchanging truth.

We need a reference that pulls together in one place the essential principles that shape a free, just, and moral society, showing that what the Church teaches is, by extension, the human truths affirmed by other religious and civil rights leaders and thinkers throughout time.

In a rightly ordered view, it's not liberal or conservative, left or right, Democrat or Republican, nor political at all, though necessarily it involves the political process. If it requires a label, call it "Dignitarian".

# Chapter 1

# Being a Dignitarian

*Man is always more than what is seen or perceived of him through experience. Failing to ask questions about man's being would lead inevitably to refusing to seek the objective truth about being as a whole, and hence, to no longer be able to recognize the basis on which human dignity, the dignity of every person, rests from the embryonic stage to natural death.*[1]

—Pope Benedict XVI

*All human beings possess in themselves (by virtue of their existence alone) the inalienable rights of life, liberty, and property ownership; no government gives these rights, and no government can take them away.*[2]

—Fr. Robert Spitzer

In his excellent book, *Ten Universal Principles*, Fr. Robert Spitzer clearly reveals the foundation of a well-ordered and civilized culture. The principles of that foundation have ancient origins, they are universal, and they concern objective truth, ethics, recognition of the dignity of men within society, and personal identity within culture. They are prerequisites for a free, just, and virtuous society, and the absence of any one of them leads to a decline in freedom, justice, and virtue in society.

[1] Pope Benedict XVI, "Address of His Holiness Benedict XVI to Participants in an Inter-academic Conference on 'The Changing Identity of the Individual'" (Jan. 28, 2008), http://www.vatican.va/holy_father/benedict_xvi/speeches/2008/january/documents/hf_ben-xvi_spe_20080128_convegno-individuo_en.html.

[2] Robert J. Spitzer, S.J., Ph.D, "Principle 7: The Principle of Natural Rights", in *Ten Universal Principles: A Brief Philosophy of the Life Issues* (San Francisco: Ignatius Press, 2011), p. 52.

"Some may say that it is the legal system or democracy or the courts that are the real protectors of individuals, culture, and society," Spitzer writes at the outset, "but ... without the ten principles, democracy could vote out the rights of human beings, court systems could legalize every form of indignity and harm, and legal systems would have nothing upon which to base their laws."[3]

Time and again, those scenarios have played out in this country, from the legalization and protection of slavery to the legalization and protection of abortion. The two are directly analogous, but that's only evident to those who see the truth clearly and recognize human subjugation however and whenever it occurs. Others, people in the abortion movement and those who support it, deceive and have been deceived by the distorted, euphemistic language of "choice" and the tortured logic of "reproductive rights" to cover for the reality of denying a class of human persons their rights.

Spitzer lists the principles of reason as the first of the ten, not by an arbitrary ordering of his own, but by the shared wisdom of Socrates, Plato, and Aristotle over two millennia ago in response to the irrational and deceitful arguments tossed out by the naysayers of their day, known as Sophists. These primary principles of reason have endured because of their truths, but sophists are still around today and continue to object to the application of reason when it counters or negates their views. Modern-day sophists work to deny natural law and moral order and revealed truth. They have a long history together with their ancient prototypes.

Take the famous Sophist Gorgias, for whom all knowledge was opinion. By his way of thinking, controlling opinion by good rhetoric makes the orator in control of knowledge itself, able to shape it to his whim. Plato shows how Socrates took him on in the dialogue simply titled *Gorgias*.

In *Abuse of Language, Abuse of Power*, Joseph Pieper noted that Plato had a lifelong battle with the Sophists, calling them "those highly paid and popularly applauded experts in the art of twisting words, who were able to sweet-talk something bad into something good and to turn white into black".[4]

[3] Ibid., p. xii.

[4] Joseph Pieper, *Abuse of Language, Abuse of Power*, trans. Lothar Krauth (San Francisco: Ignatius Press, 1992), p. 7.

If you retool the vocabulary to change or camouflage the meaning of words, *you can justify almost anything*. As Joseph Pieper put it:

> The place of authentic reality is taken over by a fictitious reality; my perception is indeed still directed toward an object, but now it is a *pseudo-reality*, deceptively appearing as being real, so much so that it becomes almost impossible anymore to discern the truth ....
>
> For the general public is being reduced to a state where people not only are unable to find out about the truth but also become unable even to *search* for the truth because they are satisfied with deception and trickery that have determined their convictions, satisfied with a fictitious reality created by design through the abuse of language.[5]

In 1998, the bishops, concerned about this moral confusion, issued *Living the Gospel of Life: A Challenge to American Catholics* (reissued in 2000). "The inherent value of human life, at every stage and in every circumstance, is not a sectarian issue any more than the Declaration of Independence is a sectarian creed", wrote the bishops.[6]

That's an excellent point, succinct and undeniable.

They wrote:

> *We cannot simultaneously commit ourselves to human rights and progress while eliminating or marginalizing the weakest among us* [my italics]. Nor can we practice the Gospel of life only as a private piety. American Catholics must live it *vigorously* and publicly, as a matter of national leadership and witness, or we will not live it at all.
>
> Bringing a respect for human dignity to practical politics can be a daunting task. There is such a wide spectrum of issues involving the protection of human life and the promotion of human dignity. Good people frequently disagree on which problems to address, which policies to adopt and how best to apply them. But for citizens and elected officials alike, the basic principle is simple: *We must begin with a commitment never to intentionally kill, or collude in the killing, of any innocent human life, no matter how broken, unformed, disabled or desperate that life may seem.*[7]

[5] Ibid., pp. 34–35.

[6] United States Conference of Catholic Bishops (USCCB), *Living the Gospel of Life: A Challenge to American Catholics* (1998), no. 20, http://www.usccb.org/issues-and-action/human-life-and-dignity/abortion/living-the-gospel-of-life.cfm.

[7] Ibid., nos. 19 and 20 (emphasis in original).

That basic principle should be, at core, one thing all people of goodwill can agree on, no matter what their faith or whether or not they profess one.

For fervent advocates of the sanctity and dignity of life for every human being, the details of political candidates' principles on life and human rights matter above all else. A health care plan or national security policy or economic strategy or a jobs plan matters only to citizens who are living in this country. And the key to that is the word *living*. How can a list of rights be declared, claimed, demanded, or defended if the first right—for a human being to live—is denied? When it is denied, the rest is incoherent.

The bishops' document warns of the urgent threat moral confusion poses to our democracy: "No one, least of all someone who exercises leadership in society, can rightfully claim to share fully and practically the Catholic faith and yet act publicly in a way contrary to that faith."[8] And yet many do.

This teaching is for them as much as for the Catholics in the pews who elect them. Again and again, the bishops restate Church teaching and fundamental moral issues for all people honestly working for human rights. And yet one election cycle after another shows how many Catholics don't apply this teaching. Who even accesses it? Who takes it seriously as opposed to as an option for a subset of Catholics?

Parsing the document for key clarifications helps. Intellectual honesty requires looking at how these moral truths line up with public policies.

> Catholic public officials are obliged to address each of these issues as they seek to build consistent policies which promote respect for the human person at all stages of life. *But being "right" in such matters can never excuse a wrong choice regarding direct attacks on innocent human life.* Indeed, *the failure to protect and defend life in its most vulnerable stages renders suspect any claims to the 'rightness' of positions in other matters affecting the poorest and least powerful of the human community* [my italics].[9]

This seems to be stating the obvious, but only to those who already see the order of priorities the Founders not only gave to the nation in their documents but also revealed as truths that preexist the State. If you can't assure the right to life, you can't claim to protect the "right" to anything a good life requires.

[8] Ibid., no. 7.

[9] Ibid., no. 22 (emphasis in original).

However, many citizens—many Christian citizens—don't see that. Shifting cultural ideology prevails over Church teaching. The bishops know that and reflect awareness of it in this document and make this incisive statement: "American Catholics have long sought to assimilate into U.S. cultural life. But in assimilating, we have too often been digested. We have been *changed* by our culture too much, and we have *changed it not enough*."[10]

That was certainly true in 2000, and it has only grown more demonstrably true since then. "Catholic public officials who disregard Church teaching on the inviolability of the human person indirectly collude in the taking of innocent life."[11] Do they think of that? We can't know or judge. But we can call on them to act according to their constituents' concerns. And we can vote, with well-formed consciences, ready and willing to apply reason to the determination of rights.

> The Gospel of Life must be proclaimed, and human life defended, in all places and all times. The arena for moral responsibility includes not only the halls of government, but the voting booth as well. *Laws that permit abortion, euthanasia and assisted suicide are profoundly unjust, and we should work peacefully and tirelessly to oppose and change them. Because they are unjust they cannot bind citizens in conscience, be supported, acquiesced in, or recognized as valid.*[12]

That is a restatement of the constant, unbroken teaching of the Church. It's a restatement of Saint Thomas Aquinas on the natural law, cited and claimed by the Rev. Dr. Martin Luther King in his Letter from Birmingham Jail. Dr. King wrote it as a response to Christian clergymen, and he opened it by answering the question of why he had come to Birmingham in the first place, since they had warned him not to bring his peaceful protestors there.

> I am in Birmingham because injustice is here. Just as the prophets of the eighth century B.C. left their villages and carried their "thus saith the Lord" far beyond the boundaries of their home towns, and just as the Apostle Paul left his village of Tarsus and carried the gospel of Jesus Christ to the far corners of the Greco Roman world, so am I compelled to carry the gospel of freedom beyond my own home town. Like Paul, I must constantly respond to the Macedonian call for aid.

[10] Ibid., no. 24 (emphasis in original).

[11] Ibid., no. 28.

[12] Ibid., no. 32 (emphasis added).

> Moreover, I am cognizant of the interrelatedness of all communities and states. I cannot sit idly by in Atlanta and not be concerned about what happens in Birmingham. Injustice anywhere is a threat to justice everywhere. We are caught in an inescapable network of mutuality, tied in a single garment of destiny. Whatever affects one directly, affects all indirectly.[13]

This is a lesson for us now. As laws affecting abortion, euthanasia, marriage, and conscience protection change in some states, laws are challenged in other states. Activists for large-scale, cultural sea change look for federal law to establish it, by government mandate or judicial fiat, as *Roe*—in one decisive stroke—nullified all fifty state laws and subsumed them under its new, and newly fabricated, right to abortion.

Dr. King continues:

> How does one determine whether a law is just or unjust? A just law is a man made code that squares with the moral law or the law of God. An unjust law is a code that is out of harmony with the moral law. To put it in the terms of Saint Thomas Aquinas: An unjust law is a human law that is not rooted in eternal law and natural law. Any law that uplifts human personality is just. Any law that degrades human personality is unjust.[14]

That applies as much to the issues of today, and it is deeply instructive.

> In the midst of a mighty struggle to rid our nation of racial and economic injustice, I have heard many ministers say: "Those are social issues, with which the gospel has no real concern." And I have watched many churches commit themselves to a completely otherworldly religion which makes a strange, un-Biblical distinction between body and soul, between the sacred and the secular.[15]

That rings so true now because it reflects the false divide today between Christians committed to "peace and social justice" and those committed to "pro-life causes", as if it's an either/or proposition instead of applying the Gospel to a "both/and" activism for the *whole life* cause of dignity and justice. This divide has a long history, and King cited it to make his point understood.

[13] Rev. Dr. Martin Luther King, Jr., "Letter from Birmingham Jail" (Apr. 16, 1963), African Studies Center, University of Pennsylvania, http://www.africa.upenn.edu/Articles_Gen/Letter_Birmingham.html, © 1963 Dr. Martin Luther King, Jr., © renewed 1991 Coretta Scott King, reprinted by arrangement with The Heirs to the Estate of Martin Luther King Jr., c/o Writers House as agent for the proprietor New York, N.Y.

[14] Ibid.

[15] Ibid.

Whenever the early Christians entered a town, the people in power became disturbed and immediately sought to convict the Christians for being "disturbers of the peace" and "outside agitators." But the Christians pressed on, in the conviction that they were "a colony of heaven," called to obey God rather than man. Small in number, they were big in commitment. They were too God-intoxicated to be "astronomically intimidated." By their effort and example they brought an end to such ancient evils as infanticide and gladiatorial contests.[16]

Many of today's Christians and secular social-justice activists have dropped the "evils of infanticide" from their causes. Even though many of them stand on the shoulders of Rev. Dr. Martin Luther King, they do not carry on the fullness of his teaching and tradition on justice and the truth of human rights "for all God's children".

His niece, Dr. Alveda King, has dedicated herself to carrying on his teaching, elaborating on his belief of inclusivity for all. If her uncle were here today, says this Dr. King, he would not claim the political views some of his avid followers ascribe to him.

In a post on Alveda King's page on the Priests for Life website, a blog devoted to her work as the group's Director of African-American Outreach, she suggests reading advice columns written by her uncle for *Ebony* magazine in 1957–1958 that reveal a man who today would be regarded as a social conservative.

"In advising men and women on questions of personal behavior 50 years ago, Uncle Martin sounded no different than a conservative Christian preacher does now," said Dr. King. "He was pro-life, pro-abstinence before marriage, and based his views on the unchanging Word of the Bible. Today, Planned Parenthood would condemn Dr. Martin Luther King, Jr., as part of the 'religious right.'"[17]

That may be a startling thought to a lot of people. But Alveda King has been saying this for decades. On another occasion honoring her uncle's memory, she issued this statement:

Martin Luther King, Jr., spoke of a Beloved Community where all are treated with respect and dignity.... He fought against society's exclusion

[16] Ibid.

[17] "Alveda King—Uncle Martin, the Social Conservative", press release, Jan. 14, 2011, Priests for Life website, http://www.priestsforlife.org/pressreleases/document-print.aspx?ID=3436.

of people who were treated as less than human because of their appearance. Today, we are compelled to continue Uncle Martin's fight by standing up for those who are treated as less than human because of their helplessness and inconvenience.

The unborn are as much a part of the Beloved Community as are newborns, infants, teenagers, adults, and the elderly. Too many of us speak of tolerance and inclusion, yet refuse to tolerate or include the weakest and most innocent among us in the human family. As we celebrate the life of Uncle Martin, let us renew our hearts and commit our lives to treating each other, whatever our race, status, or stage of life, as we would want to be treated. Let us let each other live.[18]

That, fundamentally, constitutes the civil rights movement today. It is the core of all other rights and therefore the natural extension of Rev. Dr. King's mission, carried on by his colleagues who marched at his side. One prominent colleague was Fr. Richard John Neuhaus, who summed up the legacy of the movement in a now-famous address he delivered in his final year of life. It captures the spirit, mission, and legacy of the movement Neuhaus joined King in serving. Providentially, the life cause converging with the civil rights cause is most glaringly obvious within one week of national observance each January. The federal holiday recognizing Martin Luther King Day falls within a few days of the anniversary of the infamous *Roe v. Wade* Supreme Court ruling legalizing abortion. They cannot be separated.

Neuhaus embodied the mission of the two movements as one, having marched with King and marched with the pro-life movement and speaking out for both, most eloquently in his address, "We Shall Not Weary, We Shall Not Rest".

It has been a long journey, and there are still miles and miles to go. Some say it started with the notorious *Roe v. Wade* decision of 1973 when, by what Justice Byron White called an act of raw judicial power, the Supreme Court wiped from the books of all fifty states every law protecting the unborn child. But it goes back long before that.... It goes back to the movements for eugenics and racial and ideological cleansing of the last century....

"We the People" have not and will not ratify the lethal logic of *Roe v. Wade*. That notorious decision of 1973 is the most consequential moral

[18] Alveda King, "Dr. Alveda King on King Day: The Dream Includes Us All, Born and Unborn", *Alveda King's Blog*, Jan. 18, 2010, http://www.priestsforlife.org/africanamerican/blog/index.php/dr-alveda-king-on-king-day-the-dream-includes-us-all-born-and-unborn.

> and political event of the last half century of our nation's history. It has produced a dramatic realignment of moral and political forces, led by evangelicals and Catholics together, and joined by citizens beyond numbering who know that how we respond to this horror defines who we are as individuals and as a people.[19]

That statement perfectly explains the coalition of Eastern Orthodox, Catholic, Anglican, and Evangelical religious leaders and scholars who met in Manhattan in late September 2009 to start a movement, and why they did.

## The *Manhattan Declaration*

The unique *Manhattan Declaration* is a statement and a movement based on the premise "Ours is, as it must be, a truly consistent ethic of love and life for all humans in all circumstances."[20]

Their premise is "principle over policy", the belief that social moral issues come first, and we have to get them right. Then and only then, follow policy decisions on matters like taxes, the economy, trade, and other such issues that affect the common good.

The drafters were Princeton Professor Robert P. George, Beeson Divinity School Dean Timothy George, and the late Chuck Colson of Prison Fellowship and the Colson Center. The *Manhattan Declaration* is not politically partisan. It is morally grounded in Christian values. In an exquisite economy of words, the drafters brought all important concerns about human dignity to three primary points: the sanctity of life, the preservation of traditional marriage, and the protection of conscience rights of religiously informed citizens.

### *Sanctity of Life*

"A culture of death inevitably cheapens life in all its stages and conditions by promoting the belief that lives that are imperfect, immature

[19] Richard John Neuhaus, "We Shall Not Weary, We Shall Not Rest", National Right to Life Convention, July 11, 2008, reprint, *First Things*, Jan. 22, 2013, http://www.firstthings.com/onthesquare/2013/01/we-shall-not-weary-we-shall-not-rest.

[20] *Manhattan Declaration: A Call of Christian Conscience* (Nov. 20, 2009), p. 4, http://manhattandeclaration.org/man_dec_resources/Manhattan_Declaration_full_text.pdf. This quotation also forms the banner on each webpage of the Manhattan Declaration website, http://manhattandeclaration.org/.

or inconvenient are discardable."[21] That sentence captures our society's decline over the past several decades, and those in many other countries of the world. Pope John Paul II put the term "culture of death" into popular use among people of faith in modern times, but it goes back to the *Didache*, the early Christian writing considered to be the teaching of the twelve apostles. The *Didache* begins with a teaching on *Two Ways: The Way of Life and the Way of Death*, which explicitly prohibits killing or putting a child to death by abortion or killing the child after it is born.[22]

The *Manhattan Declaration* drafters cited Mother Teresa's plea at the 1994 U.S. National Prayer Breakfast to "not kill the child" as a fundamental outcry for the "immature, inconvenient and discardable" in a society that takes recourse to the abortion license with alarming frequency. At that august event, speaking to a congregation that included political leaders who support abortion on demand, she famously said: "Please give me the child. I am willing to accept any child who would be aborted and to give that child to a married couple who will love the child and be loved by the child."

### *Dignity of Marriage*

The webpage summing up the main points of the declaration says of marriage: "The Union of one man and one woman. Marriage is the first institution of human society—indeed it is the institution on which all other human institutions have their foundation."[23]

This statement is abundantly reinforced and grounded in references Dr. Robert P. George and his coauthors cited in their book *What Is Marriage? Man and Woman: A Defense*, references that include the United Nations Convention on the Rights of the Child and numerous court rulings, which include many Supreme Court decisions.[24]

The *Manhattan Declaration* also quotes President Lyndon B. Johnson's view of the institution of marriage as primary: "When the family collapses, it is the children that are usually damaged. When it happens on a massive scale, the community itself is crippled."[25]

[21] Summary, *Manhattan Declaration* website, http://manhattandeclaration.org/#1.

[22] *Didache*, I.

[23] Summary, *Manhattan Declaration* website, http://manhattandeclaration.org/#1.

[24] Sherif Girgis, Ryan T. Anderson, and Robert P. George, *What Is Marriage? Man and Woman: A Defense* (New York: Encounter Books, 2012).

[25] Summary, *Manhattan Declaration* website, http://manhattandeclaration.org/#1.

*Freedom of Religion*

The *Manhattan Declaration*'s summary here is concise and clear again:

> No one should be compelled to embrace any religion against his will, nor should persons of faith be forbidden to worship God according to the dictates of conscience or to express freely and publicly their deeply held religious convictions.
>
> "Religious freedom, an essential requirement of the dignity of every person, is a cornerstone of the structure of human rights, and for this reason, an irreplaceable factor in the good of individuals and of the whole of society as well as of the personal fulfillment of each individual."
>
> —Pope John Paul II[26]

The Preamble of the *Manhattan Declaration* recalls Christianity's heritage:

> Christians are heirs of a 2,000-year tradition of proclaiming God's word, seeking justice in our societies, resisting tyranny, and reaching out with compassion to the poor, oppressed and suffering, ... rescuing discarded babies from trash heaps in Roman cities and publicly denouncing the Empire's sanctioning of infanticide, ... remaining in Roman cities to tend the sick and dying during the plagues, and [dying] ... rather than deny their Lord.[27]

Christian monasteries saved Western civilization after Europe was overrun by barbarian tribes, the drafters continue, preserving "not only the Bible but also the literature and art of Western culture". Christians vigorously fought the evil of slavery, with popes excommunicating anyone involved in the trade, while Evangelical Christians in England, led by John Wesley and William Wilberforce, ended slavery and "formed hundreds of societies for helping the poor, the imprisoned, and child laborers chained to machines".[28]

> In Europe, Christians challenged the divine claims of kings and successfully fought to establish the rule of law and balance of governmental powers, which made modern democracy possible. And in America, Christian women stood at the vanguard of the suffrage movement. The great civil rights crusades of the 1950s and 60s were led by Christians claiming the Scriptures and asserting the glory of the image of God in every human being regardless of race, religion, age or class.

[26] Ibid.
[27] Ibid.
[28] Ibid.

> This same devotion to human dignity has led Christians in the last decade to work to end the dehumanizing scourge of human trafficking and sexual slavery, bring compassionate care to AIDS sufferers in Africa, and assist in a myriad of other human rights causes from providing clean water in developing nations to providing homes for tens of thousands of children orphaned by war, disease and gender discrimination.[29]

This condensed history is a stark reminder of the heritage Christians carry on today and why they claim the right to continue the great tradition of fighting for human rights and defending the faith that informed such a profoundly inherent cause, the drafters declared in the Preamble. "Christians today are called to proclaim the Gospel of costly grace, to protect the intrinsic dignity of the human person and to stand for the common good. In being true to its own calling, the call to discipleship, the church through service to others can make a profound contribution to the public good."[30]

It is bold and unapologetic. It is clarity with charity. The declaration is firm and fixed on restoring moral order in the temporal order. The drafters conclude: "We will fully and ungrudgingly render to Caesar what is Caesar's. But under no circumstances will we render to Caesar what is God's."[31]

## Manhattan Declaration *Echoes U.S. Bishops' Teaching*

The three primary concerns of the *Manhattan Declaration*—"Sanctity of Life", "Dignity of Marriage", and "Freedom of Religion"—concisely subsume five major issues the United States bishops emphasize about Catholic social teaching. They are abortion, euthanasia, embryonic stem cell research, human cloning, and homosexual "marriage", all of which must be universally opposed by Catholics. First among these unchangeable principles, according to the United States bishops' document *Faithful Citizenship* (as in the *Manhattan Declaration* and the Declaration of Independence), is that of *life*.

> The consistent ethic of life provides a moral framework for principled Catholic engagement in political life and, rightly understood, neither treats all issues as morally equivalent nor reduces Catholic teaching to one

[29] Ibid.
[30] Ibid.
[31] Ibid., p. 9.

or two issues. It anchors the Catholic commitment to defend human life, from conception until natural death, in the fundamental moral obligation to respect the dignity of every person as a child of God. It unites us as a "people of life and for life" (*Evangelium Vitae*, no. 6) pledged to build what Pope John Paul II called a "culture of life" (*Evangelium Vitae*, no. 77). This culture of life begins with the preeminent obligation to protect innocent life from direct attack and extends to defending life whenever it is threatened or diminished.[32]

This teaching from the bishops is an important clarification because Catholics certainly get confused about political responsibility and the place of conscience in voting.

In 2006, a group of fifty-five Catholic members of the House of Representatives issued a "Statement of Principles" claiming a commitment to "the basic principles ... at the heart of Catholic social teaching", but refusing to accept the Church's opposition to abortion. They claimed "the primacy of conscience" as their excuse.[33]

Chicago's Cardinal George had a clear response. "A Catholic politician who excuses his or her decision to allow the killing of the unborn and of others who can't protect themselves because he or she doesn't want to 'impose Catholic doctrine on others' seems to me to be intellectually dishonest."[34]

On the basis of reason alone, he was saying, if you follow the argument through to its logical conclusion, the position doesn't hold up. "The protection of every innocent human being's right to life is a principle of reason, even though it is also a stand supported by Catholic moral teaching", he continued.

Everyone understands, by way of example, that the state should protect property by forbidding stealing. This is a matter of the common good. It is not imposing Catholic morality on anybody, even though the Church teaches that stealing is a sin. Our present legal system protects stocks and

[32] United States Conference of Catholic Bishops, *Forming Consciences for Faithful Citizenship: A Call to Political Responsibility from the Catholic Bishops of the United States* (Nov. 2007), no. 40, http://www.usccb.org/issues-and-action/faithful-citizenship/forming-consciences-for-faithful-citizenship-part-one.cfm.

[33] Nancy Frazier O'Brien, "Democrats' Statement Said to Arise from Politicians' Frustration", *Catholic News Service*, Mar. 3, 2006, http://www.catholicnews.com/data/stories/cns/0601256.htm.

[34] Francis Cardinal George, O.M.I., "Religion, Reason, Voting", *Catholic New World*, Oct. 15, 2006, http://www.catholicnewworld.com/cnwonline/2006/1015/cardinal.htm.

> bonds, as well as dogs and cats, more than it protects unborn human beings. This is contrary to the common good.[35]

As for the "primacy of conscience", Cardinal George wrote:

> Conscience is not an excuse for doing something irrational. We are to form our consciences according to the social teaching of the Church and use that formation to make political choices. This is not easy, because principles are clear but practice often is clouded by confusion of fact and the distraction of various forms of self-interest. The first and most essential principle of Catholic social teaching is the dignity of every human person and one's basic right to life from conception to natural death. Respect for human dignity is the basis for the fundamental right to life. This is a non-negotiable principle that is supported by our beliefs but is logically independent of our faith. Many non-Catholics think a society dedicated to the common good should protect its weakest members.[36]

### *A Continuation of the Civil Rights Movement*

Many are in the movement started by the *Manhattan Declaration*, and they are concerned that the definition of the "common good" has become politically malleable. "Important decisions are now being made or soon will be made [in policy and law that] ... will either uphold or undermine what is just and good", Princeton Professor Robert George told interviewer Kathryn Jean Lopez.[37]

> We believe in law and the rule of law. We recognize an obligation to comply with laws, whether we like them or not. That obligation is defeasible, however. Gravely unjust laws, and especially laws that seek to compel people to do things that are unjust, do not bind in conscience. Certainly, one must never perform a gravely unjust act, even when "following orders" or compelled by law. Christians believe—and they are far from alone in this—that one must be prepared to pay a price, sometimes a very high price indeed, for refusing to do what one's conscience tells one is wrong.[38]

[35] Ibid.

[36] Ibid.

[37] "Reminding Caesar of God's Existence: A Very Un-Manhattan-like Declaration", *National Review Online*, Dec. 1, 2009, p. 3, http://www.nationalreview.com/articles/228703/reminding-caesar-gods-existence/interview.

[38] Ibid., p. 3, http://www.nationalreview.com/articles/228703/reminding-caesar-gods-existence/interview/page/0/2?splash=.

If it came to civil disobedience in the face of gravely unjust laws, the movement set in motion by the *Manhattan Declaration* would be carrying on the tradition and cause of the civil rights movement of the 1960s, when peaceful noncompliance led to clashes with authorities. The earlier movement was considered liberal at the time, though liberalism has changed dramatically over the decades since, as has the rights movement.

The *Manhattan Declaration* movement today claims the same causes of human and civil rights, social justice, and principles that best serve the common good. Yet it has been seen as conservative. For many leaders committed to these historical causes, and many who line up in concert with them, the issues and efforts to promote and defend them transcend partisan politics. Robert George clarifies in that *National Review Online* interview:

> Actually, not all of the signatories are conservatives. Ron Sider, for example, who leads Evangelicals for Social Action, is an unabashed liberal. On matters of economics and foreign policy, he would be more comfortable in the company of the editors of *The Nation* than in the company of the editors of *National Review*. Several other signatories fall into that category. But they are strongly pro-life, pro-marriage, and pro–religious liberty. I would add that many conservatives certainly have resisted tyranny and reached out to the poor, the oppressed, and the suffering. Conservatives fought Soviet tyranny and worked for the liberation of millions of oppressed and suffering Poles, Czechs, Hungarians, Russians, Romanians, and others.
>
> Many conservatives have been in the forefront of the fight against poverty and disease in Africa, the trafficking of women and girls into sexual slavery at home and abroad, and the fight for human rights across the globe. Are there many liberals who have accomplished nearly as much as has been accomplished by the conservative activist Michael Horowitz on any of these fronts? Moreover, it is worth noting that many people who are today "conservatives" were civil-rights activists in the 1960s. Start that list with Mary Ann Glendon, Leon and Amy Kass, and the late Fr. Richard John Neuhaus. They have not changed their views about racial justice. They are today "conservatives" and no longer "liberals" because mainstream liberalism has embraced a combination of statism and moral libertarianism that they regard—rightly in my view—as deeply misguided.[39]

[39] Ibid., p. 2, http://www.nationalreview.com/articles/228703/reminding-caesar-gods-existence/interview/page/0/1.

What, after all, is a rightly ordered society? It is one that begins with recognition of and respect for the dignity of all men.

## Peace on Earth, Order in the Universe

Pope John XXIII based his 1963 Encyclical *Pacem in Terris* on the premise that mankind has always sought and longed for peace, but it "can never be established, never guaranteed, except by the diligent observance of the divinely established order".[40] The entire encyclical builds on that foundation, starting with "Order in the Universe".

> That a marvelous order predominates in the world of living beings and in the forces of nature, is the plain lesson which the progress of modern research and the discoveries of technology teach us. And it is part of the greatness of man that he can appreciate that order, and devise the means for harnessing those forces for his own benefit.
>
> But what emerges first and foremost from the progress of scientific knowledge and the inventions of technology is the infinite greatness of God Himself, who created both man and the universe ...
>
> Moreover, God created man "in His own image and likeness," endowed him with intelligence and freedom, and made him lord of creation. All this the psalmist proclaims when he says: "Thou hast made him a little less than the angels: thou hast crowned him with glory and honor, and hast set him over the works of thy hands. Thou hast subjected all things under his feet."[41]

Clearly, human dignity is preeminent. Social order is based on that principle, Pope John stated, and the human rights it yields begin with the right to life. Though he enumerated a list of others, and eloquently elaborated on them, Pope John said the common good can never exist completely unless the rights of the human person are safeguarded, starting with the first. This is quite an important and timely document, and considered so since it was issued. The idea that the Church would make this weighty pronouncement on such a modern human rights project at that time, in terms that very closely aligned with the *Universal Declaration of Human Rights*, was new.

The *Universal Declaration of Human Rights* was a magnificent document as well, with significant contributions in its drafting by French

[40] Pope John XXIII, *Pacem in Terris* (Apr. 11, 1963), no. 1, http://www.vatican.va/holy_father/john_xxiii/encyclicals/documents/hf_j-xxiii_enc_11041963_pacem_en.html.

[41] Ibid, nos. 2, 3.

Catholic philosopher Jacques Maritain. It was commissioned by the United Nations after the Second World War and went farther than the U.N. *Charter*, which reaffirmed "faith in fundamental human rights, in dignity and worth of the human person".[42] The *Universal Declaration* magnified the provisions on human rights.

Pope Benedict XVI made an apostolic visit to the United States in April 2008, primarily to address the United Nations General Assembly and observe the sixtieth anniversary of the *Universal Declaration of Human Rights*.

The pope presented the idea that there are universal values that transcend the diversity—cultural, ethnic, or ideological—embodied in an institution like the United Nations, founded to help prevent the devastation of another world war. Those values are the foundation of human rights, he said, and religion is key.[43]

He began in French, the official language of the United Nations, and only in reading the transcript do you see the rich defense he makes, repeatedly, of the dignity of the human person and the protection of the human family.

The founding principles of the organization, "the desire for peace, the quest for justice, respect for the dignity of the person, humanitarian cooperation and assistance express the just aspirations of the human spirit, and constitute the ideals which should underpin international relations", said Pope Benedict.[44]

> The United Nations embodies the aspiration for a "greater degree of international ordering" (John Paul II, *Sollicitudo Rei Socialis*, 43), inspired and governed by the principle of subsidiarity, and therefore capable of responding to the demands of the human family through binding international rules and through structures capable of harmonizing the day-to-day unfolding of the lives of peoples.[45]

First he affirmed them. Then he challenged them. "This is all the more necessary at a time when we experience the obvious paradox of a

[42] United Nations General Assembly, Preamble, *Charter of the United Nations* (June 26, 1945), http://www.un.org/en/documents/charter/preamble.shtml.

[43] Pope Benedict XVI, "Meeting with the Members of the General Assembly of the United Nations Organization: Address of His Holiness Benedict XVI" (Apr. 18, 2008), http://www.vatican.va/holy_father/benedict_xvi/speeches/2008/april/documents/hf_ben-xvi_spe_20080418_un-visit_en.html.

[44] Ibid.

[45] Ibid.

multilateral consensus that continues to be in crisis because it is still subordinated to the decisions of a few, whereas the world's problems call for interventions in the form of collective action by the international community."[46] Consensus, "decisions of a few", has replaced truth and right order, he was saying. "Recognition of the unity of the human family, and attention to the innate dignity of every man and woman, today find renewed emphasis in the principle of the responsibility to protect.... This principle has to invoke the idea of the person as image of the Creator, the desire for the absolute and the essence of freedom."[47] This snip of a substantial address is the key to his message, a rather emphatic message.

Repeatedly throughout the address, he called the United Nations to its origin and responsibility grounded in the *Universal Declaration*, and he reminded that body of the importance of the transcendent as the central reference point for human ordering in a just world.

> The founding of the United Nations, as we know, coincided with the profound upheavals that humanity experienced when *reference to the meaning of transcendence and natural reason was abandoned, and in consequence, freedom and human dignity were grossly violated*. When this happens, it threatens the objective foundations of the values inspiring and governing the international order and it undermines the cogent and inviolable principles formulated and consolidated by the United Nations. *When faced with new and insistent challenges, it is a mistake to fall back on a pragmatic approach, limited to determining "common ground"*, minimal in content and weak in its effect.[48]

They were losing their moral compass, he was telling them, and without it, they could not carry out their "duty to protect", something he repeated throughout the address. "This reference to human dignity, which is the foundation and goal of the responsibility to protect, leads us to the theme we are specifically focusing upon this year, which marks the sixtieth anniversary of the *Universal Declaration of Human Rights*."

What followed was a very important reminder:

> This document was the outcome of a convergence of different religious and cultural traditions, all of them motivated by the common desire to place the human person at the heart of institutions, laws and the workings of society, and to consider the human person essential for the world of

[46] Ibid.

[47] Ibid.

[48] Ibid. (emphasis added).

> culture, religion and science. Human rights are increasingly being presented as the common language and the ethical substratum of international relations. At the same time, the universality, indivisibility and interdependence of human rights all serve as guarantees safeguarding human dignity. It is evident, though, that the rights recognized and expounded in the *Declaration* apply to everyone by virtue of the common origin of the person, who remains the high-point of God's creative design for the world and for history. They are based on the natural law inscribed on human hearts and present in different cultures and civilizations.[49]

Though his address was widely covered by the media, they missed Pope Benedict's elegant nuances in their reporting. One hopes the members of the General Assembly did not. He parsed the issue and language of "rights" to direct attention to how they are used and misused. "Experience shows that legality often prevails over justice when the insistence upon rights makes them appear as the exclusive result of legislative enactments or normative decisions taken by the various agencies of those in power."[50]

He referred several times to the concepts of "those in power", the "majority consensus", and the "decisions of a few", and he reminded them of their duty to protect human dignity and rights. This is particularly incisive.

> When presented purely in terms of legality, rights risk becoming weak propositions divorced from the ethical and rational dimension which is their foundation and their goal. The *Universal Declaration*, rather, has reinforced the conviction that respect for human rights is principally rooted in unchanging justice, on which the binding force of international proclamations is also based. This aspect is often overlooked when the attempt is made to deprive rights of their true function in the name of a narrowly utilitarian perspective.
>
> Since rights and the resulting duties follow naturally from human interaction, it is easy to forget that they are the fruit of a commonly held sense of justice built primarily upon solidarity among the members of society, and hence valid at all times and for all peoples. This intuition was expressed as early as the fifth century by Augustine of Hippo, one of the masters of our intellectual heritage. He taught that the saying: *Do not do to others what you would not want done to you* "cannot in any way vary

[49] Ibid.

[50] Ibid.

according to the different understandings that have arisen in the world" (*De Doctrina Christiana*, III, 14). *Human rights, then, must be respected as an expression of justice, and not merely because they are enforceable through the will of the legislators.*[51]

In other words, might does not make right. That's one of the misunderstandings that have arisen in this society and throughout the world. It's going to take a lot of exposure to clear expression of sound reasoning and moral grammar to recall what we should know as true.

The universal principle of natural human rights and dignity is one of those fundamental truths. If we can make that a starting point for conversation with anyone, the understanding that all men have dignity and deserve respect, we can hope to build on that logic when we discuss the next issue of the day.

## Let's Be Clear:

1. **Certain universal principles are required for a society to be free, just, and humane.** Moral confusion over those principles threatens freedom and justice for the citizens of that society. "Human life is sacred. The dignity of the human person is the foundation of a moral vision for society."[52]
2. **All men are created with dignity and deserve to be treated accordingly.** We can't be for human rights and yet deny the most basic one that all others depend on. The right to a good life depends on the right to life. "The inherent value of human life, at every stage and in every circumstance, is not a sectarian issue any more than the Declaration of Independence is a sectarian creed."[53] "The Catholic Church proclaims that human life is sacred and that the dignity of the human person is the foundation of a moral vision for society. This belief is the foundation of all the principles of our social teaching.... We believe that every person is precious, that people are more important than things, and that the measure of every institution is whether it threatens or enhances the life and dignity of the human person."[54]

[51] Ibid. (emphasis added).

[52] USCCB, *Forming Consciences for Faithful Citizenship*, no. 44.

[53] USCCB, *Living the Gospel of Life*, no. 6.

[54] United States Conference of Catholic Bishops, "Life and Dignity of the Human Person", http://www.usccb.org/beliefs-and-teachings/what-we-believe/catholic-social-teaching/life-and-dignity-of-the-human-person.cfm.

3. **Each in his own way is called to contribute to the common good.**

> The direct duty to work for a just ordering of society ... is proper to the lay faithful. As citizens of the State, they are called to take part in public life in a personal capacity. So they cannot relinquish their participation "in the many different economic, social, legislative, administrative and cultural areas, which are intended to promote organically and institutionally the common good."[55]

> The Gospel of Life must be proclaimed, and human life defended, in all places and all times. The arena for moral responsibility includes not only the halls of government but the voting booth as well.... Every voice matters in the public forum. Every vote counts.[56]

4. **We can't claim to be Catholic and publicly contradict, reject, or betray the teachings of the faith.** Details of political candidates' principles on foundational issues such as life and human rights matter more than their party.
5. **The claim to be guided by "conscience" cannot be used as an excuse for irrational or immoral decisions.** We are to form our consciences according to the teaching of the Church and use that formation to make political choices.
6. **The "personally opposed but ... " argument is intellectually dishonest.** Some laws are inherently unjust and immoral, such as those that permit abortion, euthanasia, and assisted suicide. They can never be accepted, supported, or obeyed under the guise of political expediency or cultural compromise. Such acquiescence means compliance with gravely immoral acts.

> The consistent ethic of life provides a moral framework for principled Catholic engagement in political life and, rightly understood, neither treats all issues as morally equivalent nor reduces Catholic teaching to one or two issues. It anchors the Catholic commitment to defend human life, from conception until natural death, in the fundamental moral obligation to respect the dignity of every person as a child of God.[57]

[55] Pope Benedict XVI, *Deus Caritas Est* (2005), no. 29, quoting Pope John Paul II, *Christifideles Laici* (1988), no. 42.

[56] USCCB, *Living the Gospel of Life,* nos. 32, 33.

[57] USCCB, *Forming Consciences for Faithful Citizenship*, no. 40.

## *Chapter 2*

# Dignity from the Womb: The Beginning of Life

*The human being is to be respected and treated as a person from the moment of conception; and therefore from that same moment his rights as a person must be recognized, among which in the first place is the inviolable right of every innocent human being to life. This doctrinal reminder provides the fundamental criterion for the solution of the various problems posed by the development of the biomedical sciences in this field: since the embryo must be treated as a person, it must also be defended in its integrity, tended and cared for, to the extent possible, in the same way as any other human being as far as medical assistance is concerned.*[1]

—Congregation for the Doctrine of the Faith

*The care of human life and happiness and not their destruction is the first and only legitimate object of good government.*[2]

—Thomas Jefferson

In April 1996, Rosa Acuna was considering abortion, but was uneasy and unsure. She asked Dr. Sheldon Turkish in the six or seventh week of her pregnancy whether the baby was already there. She wanted to know whether the abortion would terminate the life of an already-existing life, or whether the procedure would prevent a human being from coming into existence in the first place. She heard the term "evacuate" and

[1] Congregation for the Doctrine of the Faith, *Donum Vitae:* Instruction on Respect for Human Life in Its Origin and on the Dignity of Procreation: Replies to Certain Questions of the Day (Feb. 22, 1987), I.1, http://www.vatican.va/roman_curia/congregations/cfaith/documents/rc_con_cfaith_doc_19870222_respect-for-human-life_en.html.

[2] Thomas Jefferson, Letter to the Republican Citizens of Washington County, Maryland, Mar. 31, 1809.

wanted to know what the abortionist would extract from her body. To her, the difference was crucial.

According to Acuna, Turkish answered, "Don't be stupid. It's only some blood." Later Turkish would claim he told her, "It's just some tissue." Based on that, she went ahead with the abortion.

The next month, she had a massive hemorrhage. Bleeding profusely, she was rushed to a hospital. Heading into the operating room on a gurney, she asked a nurse what was wrong with her. "They left part of your baby in you", the nurse told her. She'd had an incomplete abortion.

Acuna was devastated. That statement collided with what Turkish had said. In a later *New York Times Magazine* story on the case, the *Times* reported the doctor's offhanded "blob of tissue" remark to Acuna and that "she went through with the procedure only because of this lie."[3]

But afterward she decided to find the truth herself, at the local library. In medical and scientific books, Acuna came to learn that Turkish had, indeed, lied. She became severely, increasingly depressed. She sued the doctor, claiming he had had the duty to tell her she was carrying an already-existing human being.

The *Times* reported: "If what Acuna says is true, then her doctor may have breached his duty by lying to her about the basic facts of pregnancy."[4]

There are many thousands of abortions every day, millions every year. How did the *New York Times* come to report on this particular story? It was this story's unique and persistent presentation of facts that flew in the face of the accepted orthodoxy of abortion beliefs. Also of interest was its collision with another cutting-edge challenge to that orthodoxy.

For years, members of the pro-life movement had been working to establish new laws to regulate abortion clinics and their practices, such as parental notification and informed consent laws. Those efforts were always met with swift opposition from abortion providers and especially Planned Parenthood and NARAL, who generally held up or prevented those law changes.

However, a different effort was moving forward in South Dakota, with the help of pro-life attorney Harold Cassidy, a constitutional law expert whose work focuses on protecting unborn children and their

[3] Emily Bazelon, "Is There a Post-Abortion Syndrome?" *New York Times Magazine*, Jan. 21, 2007.

[4] Ibid.

mothers. The wording of the proposed new abortion counseling law in that state was crafted from Cassidy's legal writings and guided with his help. It was extraordinary in its elegant clarity.

In 2005, the legislation was passed into law by the South Dakota legislature, making it the nation's most thorough informed consent law, with wording unmatched in other such state laws. The South Dakota law required abortion clinics to tell women "that the abortion will terminate the life of a whole, separate, unique, living human being". Cassidy explained to me in an interview that the law required doctors further to tell women that abortion may cause them psychological harm. And the disclosure requirement didn't end there, because the other information abortionists were required to give was that the mother's relationship with the human being she carries is protected by the Fourteenth Amendment.

This was the biggest informed consent challenge the abortion industry had faced, and Planned Parenthood went to a U.S. District Court seeking an immediate injunction. They got one, convincing Judge Karen Schreier that the language of the informed consent law was "ideological and not biological" and therefore infringing on the abortionist's "right to free speech", Cassidy explained to me.

On appeal, a three-judge panel upheld Schreier's ruling 2–1. Cassidy explained why, noting that the opinion said "the factual underpinning" of *Roe v. Wade* was the "finding that there was no medical, scientific, or moral consensus about when life begins, making the question of when a fetus or embryo becomes a human being one of individual conscience and belief".

On the next appeal, the full Eighth Circuit Court of Appeals considered the case. In June 2008, a 7–4 majority decision threw out Schreier's order, clearing the way for the informed consent law to take effect after all. The court found that the State of South Dakota's "evidence suggests that the biological sense in which the embryo or fetus is whole, separate, unique and living should be clear in context to a physician".[5]

Acuna's suit made the case that her doctor had a duty to tell her that she was carrying life and that the embryo was an existing human

[5] United States Court of Appeals for the Eighth Circuit, *Planned Parenthood Minnesota v. Mike Rounds, Governor, and Larry Long, Attorney General,* No. 05-3093, 653 F.3d 662 (2011; submitted April 11, 2007; filed June 27, 2008), p. 19, http://www.ca8.uscourts.gov/opndir/08/06/053093P.pdf.

being. When that case headed for the New Jersey Supreme Court for review, the *New York Times Magazine* story focused on the "key issue" of whether her trial would include "evidence about the human status of the fetus". Acuna's attorneys declared that this is a medical fact. But, the *Times* noted: "The doctor's lawyers say it is a religious and philosophical question."[6]

Examining South Dakota's law by comparison was inescapable, because that law required doctors to tell women that abortion will terminate a human life already in existence instead of preventing life from coming into being.

The *Times* reported: "A federal district judge agreed with Planned Parenthood that the law would force doctors to articulate the state's viewpoint on an unsettled medical, philosophical, theological and scientific issue, that is, whether a fetus is a human being."[7]

This is not unsettled, and South Dakota did not determine when life begins, Cassidy told me. The fact of when human life begins has always been determined not by decree or edict or finding ... or "viewpoint". The blastocyst, the earliest form of life of any animal, is of the species of that animal. Planned Parenthood and other abortion activists can argue incessantly about the "personhood of the fetus". Those arguments are distractions from the main point at issue. You can't change the natural fact that human life from its conception is of the species *Homo sapiens*.

Just before the November 2008 general elections, Princeton Professor Robert P. George published a clarifying article in the *National Review Online*, entitled "When Life Begins".

> Treating the question as some sort of grand mystery, or expressing or feigning uncertainty about it, may be politically expedient, but it is intellectually indefensible. Modern science long ago resolved the question. We actually know when the life of a new human individual begins.
>
> ... From a purely biological perspective, *scientists can identify the point at which a human life begins*. The relevant studies are legion. The biological facts are uncontested. The method of analysis applied to the data is universally accepted.
>
> Your life began, as did the life of every other human being, when the fusion of egg and sperm produced a new, complete, living organism—an embryonic human being. You were never an ovum or a sperm cell, those

[6] Bazelon, "Is There a Post-Abortion Syndrome?"
[7] Ibid.

were both functionally and genetically parts of other human beings—your parents. But you *were* once an embryo, just as you were once an adolescent, a child, an infant, and a fetus. By an internally directed process, you developed from the embryonic stage into and through the fetal, infant, child, and adolescent stages of development and ultimately into adulthood with your determinateness, unity, and identity fully intact. You are the same being—the same *human* being—who once was an embryo....

In view of the established facts ... the real question is not whether human beings in the embryonic and fetal stages *are* human beings. *Plainly they are.* The question is whether we will honor or abandon our civilizational and national commitment to the equal worth and dignity of all human beings—even the smallest, youngest, weakest, and most vulnerable.[8]

Again, that was just prior to the November 2008 presidential election, which resulted in the most pro-abortion president in U.S. history to occupy the White House.

How did this nation get to that point?

An editorial in the journal of the California Medical Association shows how. Succinctly, it reveals the strategy it would take to make the unacceptable become socially acceptable.

The CMA admitted the traditional Western ethic had always placed great intrinsic value and worth on every human life at all stages, and that ethic had always been embraced and held sacred by the Judeo-Christian heritage of this country, making it the basis for most laws and social policies. But then the CMA turned a corner, arguing that a population explosion timed with "ecological disparity" compounded by the "quality of life" issue combined with "unprecedented technologic progress and achievement" have all together posed "new facts and social realities", ones the editors felt were "within the power of humans to control".[9] They tipped their hand right there. But then they swung for the fences.

It will become necessary and acceptable to place relative rather than absolute values on such things as human lives ... Since the old ethic has not yet been fully displaced it has been necessary to separate the idea of

[8] Robert P. George, "When Life Begins: Will Politics Trump Science?" *National Review Online*, Nov. 2, 2008, http://www.nationalreview.com/articles/226168/when-life-begins/robert-p-george (emphasis in original).

[9] California Medical Association, "A New Ethic for Medicine and Society", *California Medicine* 113, no. 3 (Sept. 1970): 67–68.

> abortion from the idea of killing, which continues to be socially abhorrent. The result has been a curious avoidance of the scientific fact, which everyone really knows, that human life begins at conception and is continuous whether intra- or extra-uterine until death. The very considerable semantic gymnastics which are required to rationalize abortion as anything but taking a human life would be ludicrous if they were not often put forth under socially impeccable auspices. It is suggested that this schizophrenic sort of subterfuge is necessary because while a new ethic is being accepted the old one has not yet been rejected.[10]

What to say ... That *this was Orwellian* is just cliché.

The editorial went on to anticipate "birth control and birth selection [extending] inevitably to death selection and death control whether by the individual or by society, [causing] public and professional determinations of when and when not to use scarce resources".[11]

The 1970 editorial ended on this foreboding note: "It is not too early for our profession to examine this new ethic ... and prepare to apply it in a rational development for the fulfillment and betterment of mankind in what is almost certain to be a biologically oriented world society."[12]

Rational? This tortured logic could justify a new system for a "biologically oriented world society"? What does that mean? By what measure does that constitute the betterment of mankind? What, exactly, does it fulfill? Who decides that?

Ah, but that's the question.

## Who Decides?

The entire abortion movement, which turned forty-one January 22, 2014, anniversary of the Supreme Court *Roe* decision, but much older in practice, always turned on the premise that a woman has "the right to choose" what happens to, with, and in her own body. But that's been a smoke screen—an enduring and successful one—for decades. It's based on the false premise that a pregnant woman is a container carrying a part she can arbitrarily dispose of if it's inconvenient for her.

And it doesn't cover the truth.

[10] Ibid., p. 68.
[11] Ibid.
[12] Ibid.

In 1995, feminist author Naomi Wolf published a controversial article, "Our Bodies, Our Souls: Re-thinking Pro-Choice Rhetoric". Here's some of what she said:

> At its best, feminism defends its moral high ground by being simply faithful to the truth: to women's real-life experiences. But to its own ethical and political detriment, the pro-choice movement has relinquished the moral frame around the issue of abortion. It has ceded the language of right and wrong to abortion foes. The movement's abandonment of what Americans have always, and rightly, demanded of their movements—an ethical core—and its reliance instead on a political rhetoric in which the foetus means nothing are proving fatal.
>
> The effects of this abandonment can be measured in two ways. First of all, such a position causes us to lose political ground. By refusing to look at abortion within a moral framework, we lose the millions of Americans who want to support abortion as a legal right but still need to condemn it as a moral iniquity. Their ethical allegiances are then addressed by the pro-life movement, which is willing to speak about good and evil.
>
> But we are also in danger of losing something more important than votes; we stand in jeopardy of losing what can only be called our souls. Clinging to a rhetoric about abortion in which there is no life and no death, we entangle our beliefs in a series of self-delusions, fibs and evasions. And we risk becoming precisely what our critics charge us with being: callous, selfish and casually destructive men and women who share a cheapened view of human life.[13]

This was rare, soul-searching honesty from a pro-choice feminist. But the most poignant honesty was yet to come.

> Any doubt that our current pro-choice rhetoric leads to disaster should be dispelled by the famous recent defection of ... the woman who had been Jane Roe....What happened to Norma McCorvey? To judge by her characterisation in the elite media and by some prominent pro-choice feminists, nothing very important. Her change of heart about abortion was relentlessly "explained away" as having everything to do with fickleness and little to do with any actual moral agency....
>
> To me, the first commandment of real feminism is: when in doubt, listen to women. What if we were to truly, respectfully listen to this woman

[13] Naomi Wolf, "Our Bodies, Our Souls: Re-thinking Pro-Choice Rhetoric", *New Republic*, 1995; republished as "Naomi Wolf on Abortion: 'Our Bodies, Our Souls' ", *New Statesman*, Jan. 27, 2013, http://www.newstatesman.com/politics/politics/2013/01/archive-naomi-wolfs-our-bodies-our-souls.

> who began her political life as, in her words, just "some little old Texas girl who got in trouble"? We would have to hear this: perhaps Norma McCorvey actually had a revelation that she could no longer live as the symbol of a belief system she increasingly repudiated.
>
> McCorvey should be seen as an object lesson for the pro-choice movement—a call to us to search our souls and take another, humbler look at how we go about what we are doing. For McCorvey is in fact an American Everywoman: she is the lost middle of the abortion debate, the woman whose allegiance we forfeit by our refusal to use a darker and sterner and more honest moral rhetoric.[14]

So honest was Norma McCorvey's humbling, soul-searching desire for truth that she followed it into the pro-life movement and the Catholic Church.

Wolf's article continued into "personhood" and constitutional provisions for "persons", parsing terms. But the constitutional law expert behind both the Rosa Acuna case and the South Dakota informed consent law, and its defense, has no patience for what he considers meaningless arguments. Harold Cassidy minces no words: "The more fundamental issue is *this*", he says, with no-nonsense gravity. "Either a human being has certain rights or they don't."

By forcing the case through the appeals process, Cassidy explained, Planned Parenthood essentially asked the court to decide this: "Does abortion kill a human being?"

The last and final ruling on the South Dakota informed consent law came in July 2012. The full Eighth Circuit Court upheld the law requiring that a woman seeking a lawful abortion in the state be advised of the following:

1. That the abortion will terminate the life of a whole, separate, unique, living human being in a scientific sense (the human being disclosure).
2. That the patient has an existing relationship with that unborn human being protected by law, which will be terminated by having an abortion (the relationship advisories).
3. A description of all known medical risks of the abortion procedure, including the increased risk of suicide or "suicide ideation" (medical risk disclosure).[15]

[14] Ibid.

[15] See *Planned Parenthood Minnesota v. Rounds*, pp. 51–53.

"These risk factors are where the debate is today", said Cassidy. "This forced the courts to look at issues in a way they never have before." They had to deliberate on the science of life and the case law weighing historically in favor of a mother's right to her relationship with her unborn child.

## The Gosnell Trial: Murders in an Abortion Clinic

In Spring 2013, a court was forced to look at abortion issues in yet another new way in the lengthy trial of late-term abortionist Kermit Gosnell. He was charged with the murder of a woman during a botched abortion and the murder of seven babies who had been born alive. The grand jury report was detailed and graphic:

> When you perform late-term "abortions" by inducing labor, you get babies. Live, breathing, squirming babies. By 24 weeks, most babies born prematurely will survive if they receive appropriate medical care. But that was not what the Women's Medical Society was about. Gosnell had a simple solution for the unwanted babies he delivered: he killed them. He didn't call it that. He called it "ensuring fetal demise." The way he ensured fetal demise was by sticking scissors into the back of the baby's neck and cutting the spinal cord. He called that "snipping."
>
> Over the years, there were hundreds of "snippings." Sometimes, if Gosnell was unavailable, the "snipping" was done by one of his fake doctors, or even by one of the administrative staff. But all the employees of the Women's Medical Society knew. Everyone there acted as if it wasn't murder at all.
>
> Most of these acts cannot be prosecuted, because Gosnell destroyed the files. Among the relatively few cases that could be specifically documented, one was Baby Boy A. His 17-year-old mother was almost 30 weeks pregnant—seven and a half months—when labor was induced. An employee estimated his birth weight as approaching six pounds. He was breathing and moving when Dr. Gosnell severed his spine and put the body in a plastic shoebox for disposal.... Another, Baby Boy B, whose body was found at the clinic frozen in a one-gallon spring-water bottle, was at least 28 weeks of gestational age when he was killed. Baby C was moving and breathing for 20 minutes before an assistant came in and cut the spinal cord, just the way she had seen Gosnell do it so many times.
>
> And these were not even the worst cases.[16]

[16] Report of the Grand Jury in the Court of Common Pleas, First Judicial District of Pennsylvania, Criminal Trial Division, in re: MISC. NO. 0009901-2008, County Investigating: Grand Jury XXIII; Section I: Overview; Filed January 2011; *City of Philadelphia Online*, http://www.phila.gov/districtattorney/pdfs/grandjurywomensmedical.pdf.

The logic of abortion, carried through to its ultimate conclusion, was on trial. And the verdict of the People was: Guilty. As NBC news in Philadelphia reported, Gosnell was found guilty of "first-degree murder in the deaths of three babies authorities said were born alive before having their necks cut with scissors.... In addition to the murder charges, the 72-year-old was found guilty Monday of involuntary manslaughter in the overdose death of former patient Karnamaya Mongar."[17] It's sad it had to take such horrific circumstances to admit what's always been true: that it's "babies" and women who are the victims in abortion clinics.

The case marked a turning point unprecedented in the forty years after *Roe v. Wade*. People who had identified themselves as pro-choice all along publicly admitted that the Gosnell trial forced them to reconsider the very premise of their belief about the right to abortion on demand. It forced us to look at what abortion is, and what abortion does. Not every abortionist is a Kermit Gosnell, but every abortionist ends a human life.

## The Slavery/Abortion Analogy

Abraham Lincoln forged the Emancipation Proclamation to free slaves in 1863 and wrestled with Congress to get it ratified in the Thirteenth Amendment two years later and abolish slavery for good, for those freed from bondage "and for millions yet unborn". He couldn't have imagined a future United States Supreme Court ruling that would render an entire class of human beings unworthy of constitutional protection, nor a government that would back it in funding and law. Only this time, the class of human beings in bondage and under the control of others could be legally killed if the one who controlled their fate so chose. And that decider was the mother.

Slavery and abortion are directly analogous.

Consider this ...

In the 2008 presidential campaign, popular Evangelical Christian Pastor Rick Warren moderated the Saddleback Civil Forum in which he questioned Democratic candidate Senator Barack Obama and Republican candidate Senator John McCain, one on one, with the other candidate backstage and unable to hear. Neither candidate knew what he

[17] Vince Lattanzio, "Abortion Doctor Gosnell Found Guilty of Killing 3 Babies Born Alive", *NBC-10 Philadelphia Online*, May 14, 2013, http://www.nbcphiladelphia.com/news/local/Gosnell-Murder-Deliberations-Stretch-into-10th-Day-207178491.html.

would be asked, and both were asked the identical set of questions. Here's a snip:

> WARREN: Now, let's deal with abortion; 40 million abortions since Roe v. Wade. As a pastor, I have to deal with this all of the time, all of the pain and all of the conflicts. I know this is a very complex issue. Forty million abortions, at what point does a baby get human rights, in your view?
>
> OBAMA: Well, you know, I think that whether you're looking at it from a theological perspective or a scientific perspective, answering that question with specificity, you know, is above my pay grade.[18]

Mr. Obama turned the question of when a baby gets human rights into a question of when human life begins. The facts are available in any medical textbook and undeniable even without a medical degree that human life begins at conception (which Rosa Acuna found out, and the Eighth Circuit Court of Appeals decision had already recognized in law by the time of the Saddleback Forum). So the question of when human life begins, raised by Mr. Obama in response to the actual question, is answerable, and easily.

By responding as he did, Mr. Obama avoided the question of when a baby gets rights. His record as senator in Illinois shows that he denied babies who survived abortion attempts any rights under law. When asked about his reticence to support bills that protect these infants, Obama's reason was incredible.

> Number one ... whenever we define a pre-viable fetus as a person that is protected by the Equal Protection Clause or the other elements in the Constitution, what we're really saying is, in fact, that they are persons that are entitled to the kinds of protections that would be provided to a—a child, a 9-month old—child that was delivered to term. That determination then, essentially, if it was accepted by a court, would forbid abortions to take place. I mean, it—it would essentially bar abortions, because the Equal Protection Clause does not allow somebody to kill a child, and if this is a child, then this would be an anti-abortion statute.[19]

[18] "Saddleback Presidential Candidates Forum", aired Aug. 16, 2008, *Transcripts: CNN.com*, http://transcripts.cnn.com/TRANSCRIPTS/0808/16/se.02.html.

[19] As cited in Terence P. Jeffery, "Obama Is the Most Pro-Abortion Candidate Ever", *CNSNews.com*, Mar. 4, 2009, http://cnsnews.com/blog/terence-p-jeffrey/obama-most-pro-abortion-candidate-ever.

This is the same argument that was used by proponents of slavery, upheld in the Supreme Court *Dred Scott* decision. If slaves were to be accepted and regarded as persons, then they would be entitled to the same constitutional protections provided to whites. Thus legislation would have to forbid slavery, because the Constitution protects the life and liberty of all persons, since we are all created equal.

How did the pro-abortion argument gain such currency?

Former abortionist Dr. Bernard Nathanson tried to explain. In failing health, about two years before he died, he taped a video for the South Dakota "Women's Health and Infant Protection Act" (technically known as Initiated Measure 11).

> I am Dr. Bernard Nathanson, formerly director of the largest abortion facility in the Western world, and the last surviving founder of NARAL, the pro-abortion organization we founded in New York City in the late 1960s. We founded NARAL to export our pro-abortion mentality across the land.
>
> One of our strategies in order to mislead the American public was to deny what we knew to be true, that abortion kills an existing human being. We denied that fact in an effort to mislead the American public and the courts of this land.
>
> I myself am personally responsible for over 75,000 abortions. This was the greatest mistake of my life, and legal abortion was the greatest mistake this nation has ever conceived. It must be brought to an end after 50 million deaths of unborn babies.
>
> I am Dr. Bernard Nathanson, Obstetrician/Gynecologist and the last surviving member of the NARAL group. The people of South Dakota can end the use of abortion as birth control in their state by voting yes on issue 11 on November 4.[20]

How can the two greatest mistakes this nation has ever conceived, slavery and abortion, be so analogous and yet so disparately viewed? Slavery was a heinous, vile, immoral, brutal, and inhumane scourge on our national conscience. But abortion is too, though it's considered by a large part of this same nation to be a "right", a preeminent right that brings "reproductive justice" and equal rights to balance the social scale.

We need perspective.

[20] Bernard Nathanson, "Last Surviving Founding Member of NARAL", video, Sept. 19, 2008, http://www.youtube.com/watch?v=1xfEoqGeliA.

## The Right That Precedes All Other Rights

Three students coauthored an opinion piece in the Massachusetts Institute of Technology online publication *The Tech* in November 2010 entitled "The Fundamental Right to Life" as a rebuttal to an article suggesting that abortion is "a question of values". The students point to the Declaration of Independence as the authoritative source of guaranteed rights and their ordering. Here's a portion of their argument:

> Simply by virtue of being human, all human beings are "endowed by their Creator with certain unalienable Rights." ...
>
> ... [I]f we return to the words of the Declaration of Independence, "among these [rights] are Life, Liberty and the pursuit of Happiness," we find [a] cardinal ordering of rights ... : without Life one cannot exercise Liberty, and without Liberty one cannot pursue Happiness. The right to life is a prerequisite for all other rights. Thus, the right to life is the fundamental human right....
>
> To deny the fundamental nature of the right to life is to deny the basis of all human rights. If ... we were to accept the assignment of arbitrary precedence to human rights, we then must permit the justification of any infringement upon the rights of another. In a society where anyone can elevate their right to liberty or property or religion above another's right to live, the weak are helpless before those who are able to assert their rights more strongly....
>
> Above all, we wish to emphasize that every human being, in every stage of life, has a fundamental and unalienable right to life which serves as the foundation for all other human rights in a just society. The right to life is granted by neither state nor men, but it is their duty to protect it.[21]

The principles eloquently stated in the Declaration of Independence are identical to the thought, tradition, and teaching of the Catholic Church on the equality of all men, with rights that come from God and preexist the State, on the role of government to function for the common good, and on its source of power lying in the consent of the governed.

In his 1963 Encyclical *Pacem in Terris*, Pope John XXIII addressed an array of timely realities and eternal truths, covering these issues of rights,

[21] Elise McCall, Matt Shireman, and Tony Valderrama, "Opinion: The Fundamental Right to Life", *The Tech: Online Edition* 130, no. 50 (Nov. 2, 2010), http://tech.mit.edu/V130/N50/fundright.html.

duties, nations, individuals, women, and the emerging consciousness of human dignity. The chosen topic of the encyclical is peace, and Pope John says that can only be found in justice and moral order founded on truth.

> But first We must speak of man's rights. Man has the right to live. He has the right to bodily integrity and to the means necessary for the proper development of life, particularly food, clothing, shelter, medical care, rest, and, finally, the necessary social services. In consequence, he has the right to be looked after in the event of ill health; disability stemming from his work; widowhood; old age; enforced unemployment; or whenever through no fault of his own he is deprived of the means of livelihood.[22]

Now these assorted rights have been convoluted and separated out by some Christians to focus on certain rights at the expense of others, which was the opposite of Pope John's intention in this teaching.

## Priority of Issues

This is the essence of the teaching of the United States Conference of Catholic Bishops (USCCB) in the bishops' 2007 document *Forming Consciences for Faithful Citizenship* on the key social moral issues of our time. They apply the timeless teaching of the Church to inform Catholics who engage in the political process. It transcends religious affiliation.

> What faith teaches about the dignity of the human person and about the sacredness of every human life helps us see more clearly the same truths that also come to us through the gift of human reason. At the center of these truths is respect for the dignity of every person. This is the core of Catholic moral and social teaching. Because we are people of both faith and reason, it is appropriate and necessary for us to bring this essential truth about human life and dignity to the public square.[23]

Individual bishops have made that case well and in their own way. In an October 2008 column in the *Saint Louis Review*, Bishop Robert Hermann put it succinctly: "Today we are concerned about the economic

[22] Pope John XXIII, *Pacem in Terris* (Apr. 11, 1963), no. 11.

[23] USCCB, *Forming Consciences for Faithful Citizenship: A Call to Political Responsibility from the Catholic Bishops of the United States*, "Part I: The U.S. Bishops' Reflection on Catholic Teaching and Political Life" (Nov. 2007), no. 10, http://www.usccb.org/issues-and-action/faithful-citizenship/forming-consciences-for-faithful-citizenship-part-one.cfm.

collapse of our country. We should be far more concerned about the spiritual collapse of our country.... We have heard the word 'abortion' so often that perhaps we no longer associate procured abortion with the killing of children, yet that is what it is."[24] That same month, then–New York Archbishop, Cardinal Edward Egan, elaborated emotionally on that point in a column published with a large, color photo of a baby in the womb. Under the title "Just Look" was this: "The picture on this page is an untouched photograph of a being that has been within its mother for 20 weeks. Please do me the favor of looking at it carefully."[25] Then he makes an impassioned case.

> Have you any doubt that it is a human being?
>
> If you do not have any such doubt, have you any doubt that it is an *innocent* human being? If you have no doubt about this either, have you any doubt that the authorities in a civilized society are duty-bound to protect this innocent human being if anyone were to wish to kill it?
>
> If you have no doubt that the authorities in a civilized society would be duty-bound to protect this innocent human being if someone were to wish to kill it, I would suggest—even insist—that there is not a lot more to be said about the issue of abortion in our society. It is wrong, and it cannot—must not—be tolerated.
>
> But you might protest that all of this is too easy.... Why do I neglect philosophers and theologians? Why do I not get into defining "human being," "person," "living," and the rest? Because, I respond, I am sound of mind and endowed with a fine set of eyes, into which I do not believe it is well to cast sand....
>
> But what about the being that has been in its mother for only 15 weeks or only 10? Have you photographs of that too? Yes, I do. However, I hardly think it necessary to show them.... If there is a time when something less than a human being in a mother morphs into a human being, it is not a time that anyone has ever been able to identify, though many have made guesses....
>
> If you can convince yourself that these beings are something other than living and innocent human beings (perhaps "mere clusters of tissues," as one national newsmagazine suggests), you have a problem far

[24] Bishop Robert Hermann, "I Thought You Should Know", *Saint Louis Review*, Oct. 10, 2008, http://stlouisreview.com/article/2008-10-01/bishop-hermann-i.

[25] Edward Cardinal Egan, "Cardinal's Column: Just Look", Archdiocese of New York, Oct. 23, 2008, http://www.archny.org/news-events/columns-and-blogs/cardinals-monthly-column/index.cfm?i=9314.

> more basic than merely not appreciating the wrongness of abortion. And that problem is—forgive me—self-deceit in a most extreme form....
>
> One day, please God, when the stranglehold on public opinion in the United States has been released by the extremists for whom abortion is the center of their political and moral life, our nation will, in my judgment, look back on what we have been doing to innocent human beings within their mothers as a crime no less heinous than what was approved by the Supreme Court in the "Dred Scott Case" in the 19th century, and no less heinous than what was perpetrated by Hitler and Stalin in the 20th. There is nothing at all complicated about the utter wrongness of abortion, and making it all seem complicated mitigates that wrongness not at all. On the contrary, it intensifies it.[26]

This is clarifying.

At that same time, the U.S. bishops released a joint statement by Cardinal Justin Rigali and Bishop William Murphy on the *Faithful Citizenship* guide of 2007 (later revised) and the bishops' intention in drafting it to help Catholic voters form their consciences in line with the Church's moral teaching. "We emphasized that: 'Both opposing evil and doing good are essential obligations.' Unfortunately, there seem to be efforts and voter education materials designed to persuade Catholics that they need only choose one approach: either opposing evil or doing good. This is not an authentically Catholic approach."[27]

Cardinal Francis George was president of the USCCB then, and he reflected that same frustration in an interview with former *National Catholic Reporter*'s journalist John Allen. "If you've got an immoral law, you've got to work to change that", said Cardinal George. "That's the great scandal, and that's why there's such a sense of urgency now. There's no recognition of the fact that children continue to be killed, and we live, therefore, in a country drenched in blood. This can't be something that you start playing off pragmatically against other issues."[28]

It's interesting that Cardinal George said, "that's why there's such a sense of urgency now". In 1963, when Dr. Martin Luther King delivered

[26] Ibid.

[27] Cardinal Justin Rigali, Chairman, Committee on Pro-Life Activities, and Bishop William Murphy, Chairman, Committee on Domestic Justice and Human Development, USCCB, "Joint Statement on *Faithful Citizenship*" (Oct. 21, 2008), http://www.paxjoliet.org/news/joint_statement_election_2008.htm.

[28] John L. Allen, Jr., "Synod: Interview with Cardinal Francis George", *National Catholic Reporter,* Oct. 15, 2008, http://ncronline.org/news/synod-interview-cardinal-francis-george.

his most famous speech, "I Have a Dream", he referred to "the fierce urgency of Now". One hundred years after the Emancipation Proclamation, he lamented that actual freedom was still not in the reach or grasp of black Americans.

> In a sense we've come to our nation's capital to cash a check. When the architects of our republic wrote the magnificent words of the Constitution and the Declaration of Independence, they were signing a promissory note to which every American was to fall heir. This note was a promise that all men, yes, black men as well as white men, would be guaranteed the "Unalienable Rights of Life, Liberty and the pursuit of Happiness." It is obvious today that America has defaulted on this promissory note, insofar as her citizens of color are concerned. Instead of honoring this sacred obligation, America has given the Negro people a bad check, a check which has come back marked "insufficient funds."
>
> But we refuse to believe that the bank of justice is bankrupt. We refuse to believe that there are insufficient funds in the great vaults of opportunity of this nation. And so, we've come to cash this check, a check that will give us upon demand the riches of freedom and the security of justice.
>
> We have also come to this hallowed spot to remind America of the fierce urgency of now....[29]

Many Catholic clergy and faithful joined King's civil rights movement, and they continue the same social activism for freedom and justice in what they consider the new civil rights movement, the right to life. That includes his niece, Dr. Alveda King, Director of African-American Outreach at Priests for Life, and founder of the King for America organization. "The babies need us", Alveda King said on the occasion of a March for Life rally. "You know, they're like a slave in the womb of a mom. The mom's deciding whether they will live or die. It's civil rights."[30] King said supporting so-called "abortion rights" contradicts the nonviolence to which her uncle dedicated his life in the civil rights movement he led.

Alveda King had two abortions herself, one before *Roe* legalized it and one afterward. When she planned to have a third abortion, "she

[29] Dr. Martin Luther King, Jr., "I Have a Dream", Address delivered at the March on Washington for Jobs and Freedom, Washington, D.C., Aug. 28, 1963; transcript by *PBS Newshour*, http://www.pbs.org/newshour/extra/teachers/lessonplans/english/mlk_transcript.pdf, © 1963 Dr. Martin Luther King, Jr., © renewed 1991 Coretta Scott King, reprinted by arrangement with The Heirs to the Estate of Martin Luther King Jr., c/o Writers House as agent for the proprietor New York, N.Y.

[30] "Niece of Late Civil Rights Leader Addresses Anti-abortion Crowd", *Boston's Channel 7 News WHDH*, Jan. 27, 2007, http://www1.whdh.com/news/articles/local/BO41364.

was urged by two African-American men, her grandfather, the father of Martin Luther King, Jr., and her boyfriend, not to. 'A woman has a right to choose what she does with her body, of course she does. But I had to admit right then that baby was not my body,' she said. 'I did not have the right to kill another person.' "[31]

## Principle and Policy

The right to life is the first unalienable right held as a self-evident truth in the Declaration of Independence. That is the first of three foundational principles of justice defended in the *Manhattan Declaration*. And it is also the first of several other crucial principles the Catholic Church teaches on participation in political life, principles sometimes referred to as "non-negotiable".

That has caused some inflammatory rhetoric within the Catholic media world as progressives and conservatives go back and forth on the politics of terminology. The Church teaches that good Catholics can disagree on matters of prudential judgment, such as how to apply certain "non-negotiable" principles in any given policy. But they cannot disagree on the principles themselves, if they involve ending human life, altering marriage, or denying religious freedom.

Progressives say the language is a thinly disguised promotion of a GOP agenda, and that Catholic teaching has plenty more than a few or handful of teachings that are "intrinsically evil and not negotiable". Progressives say conservatives are overlooking issues of poverty, just war, human trafficking, arbitrary imprisonment, unjust work conditions, and so on. Conservatives respond that politicians don't openly advocate subhuman living conditions, or call for arbitrary imprisonments, or attend fundraisers for the human-trafficking industry, or endorse government subsidies for prostitution, or demand legal protection for slavery. But politicians do openly support abortion, same-sex marriage, sometimes embryonic stem cell research (which terminates human life), and the mandate to violate beliefs protected by the First Amendment in order to provide for abortion-inducing drugs and procedures.

This needs continual clarity.

In his Apostolic Exhortation *Christifideles Laici*—Pope John Paul II's letter to the laity on their mission in the Church and the world—he

[31] Ibid.

strongly urged them to defend life as a foundation for other work in carrying out the Church's social gospel.

> The inviolability of the person, which is a reflection of the absolute inviolability of God, finds its primary and fundamental expression in the inviolability of human life. Above all, the common outcry, which is justly made on behalf of human rights—for example, the right to health, to home, to work, to family, to culture—is false and illusory if the right to life, the most basic and fundamental right and the condition for all other personal rights, is not defended with maximum determination.[32]

If we cannot guarantee protection of the right to life, we can't make a coherent argument for other rights that depend on that first, most basic one.

Pope Benedict spoke to European Parliamentarians on these issues in a March 2006 address, and on why he and the Church in general raise them with citizens and leaders of nations. Here's part of what he said:

> As far as the Catholic Church is concerned, the principal focus of her interventions in the public arena is the protection and promotion of the dignity of the person, and she is thereby consciously drawing particular attention to principles which are not negotiable. Among these the following emerge clearly today:
>
> - protection of life in all its stages, from the first moment of conception until natural death;
> - recognition and promotion of the natural structure of the family—as a union between a man and a woman based on marriage—and its defence from attempts to make it juridically equivalent to radically different forms of union which in reality harm it and contribute to its destabilization, obscuring its particular character and its irreplaceable social role;
> - the protection of the right of parents to educate their children.
>
> These principles are not truths of faith, even though they receive further light and confirmation from faith; they are inscribed in human nature itself and therefore they are common to all humanity. The Church's action in promoting them is therefore not confessional in character, but is addressed to all people, prescinding from any religious affiliation they

[32] Pope John Paul II, Post-Synodal Apostolic Exhortation *Christifideles Laici* (Dec. 30, 1988), no. 38.

> may have. On the contrary, such action is all the more necessary the more these principles are denied or misunderstood, because this constitutes an offence against the truth of the human person, a grave wound inflicted onto justice itself.[33]

In his 2009 Encyclical *Caritas in Veritate*, Pope Benedict continued to address the primacy of life.

> The Church forcefully maintains this link between life ethics and social ethics, fully aware that "a society lacks solid foundations when, on the one hand, it asserts values such as the dignity of the person, justice and peace, but then, on the other hand, radically acts to the contrary by allowing or tolerating a variety of ways in which human life is devalued and violated, especially where it is weak or marginalized."[34]

The ethic of life is consistent, but the need to repeat it is urgent and persistent. Why? Popes, bishops, and religious leaders of Christian denominations and the Orthodox church, Jewish scholars and rabbis, and even Atheists for Life speak out for this first right every chance they get. But there is still an entrenched "abortion rights" movement that does not hear, or see.

## A Voice for the Voiceless

Some pro-life leaders say many people won't reject abortion until they see abortion. For some, it takes that or, like Rosa Acuna, learning what happens in an abortion. And then they will oppose it and try to stop it from happening to other women and their children.

Abby Johnson grew up in a Christian family with pro-life beliefs, but she gradually wound up working with Planned Parenthood, starting in college and ascending the ranks to director of one of their clinics. She knew what happened there, but it wasn't until she saw it firsthand in an unexpected confrontation that she faced the truth of it all. Instead of sitting behind a desk or talking with patients or doing paperwork, she was called into the examination room to assist in an ultrasound-guided

[33] Pope Benedict XVI, "Address of His Holiness Benedict XVI to the Members of the European People's Party on the Occasion of the Study Days on Europe" (Mar. 30, 2006), http://www.vatican.va/holy_father/benedict_xvi/speeches/2006/march/documents/hf_ben-xvi_spe_20060330_eu-parliamentarians_en.html.

[34] Pope Benedict XVI, *Caritas in Veritate* (June 29, 2009), no. 15, citing Pope John Paul II, *Evangelium Vitae* (Mar. 25, 1995), no. 101.

abortion, holding the probe. "I could not have imagined how the next ten minutes would shake the foundation of my values and change the course of my life", she wrote.[35]

And then she explains, in a brief, breathtaking account of that moment in her book *UnPlanned*, that she saw "the entire, perfect profile of a baby ... the head, both arms, legs, and even tiny fingers and toes".[36] The child looked absolutely perfect at that twelve-week age, and she was riveted by this image of a perfectly formed baby on the ultrasound screen. "'Okay,' the doctor said, looking at me, 'just hold the probe in place during the procedure so I can see what I'm doing.'"[37]

Then he inserted the tube—the cannula—that would suction out that baby, whole and entire, in mere moments. "It gently probed the baby's side.... The next movement was the sudden jerk of a tiny foot as the baby started kicking, as if trying to move away from the probing invader. As the cannula pressed in, the baby began struggling to turn and twist away."[38] And then the doctor called for the suction to be turned on.

> The cannula was already being rotated by the doctor, and now I could see the tiny body violently twisting with it. For the briefest moment it looked as if the baby were being wrung like a dishcloth, twirled and squeezed. And then the little body crumpled and began disappearing into the cannula before my eyes. The last thing I saw was the tiny, perfectly formed backbone sucked into the tube, and then everything was gone. And the uterus was empty. Totally empty.[39]

When she recovered from the shock, Abby realized that what her husband had said in the past had been right: when a woman wants the child, it's a baby; when she doesn't, it's a fetus. But it was alive and fighting for life, and she saw the whole thing. Seeing that baby lose a battle to live "in the blink of an eye" changed Abby Johnson that instant. "*What I have told people for years, what I've believed and taught and defended, is a lie.*"[40]

[35] Abby Johnson, *UnPlanned: The Dramatic True Story of a Former Planned Parenthood Leader's Eye-Opening Journey across the Life Line* (San Francisco: Ignatius Press, 2011), p. 3.

[36] Ibid.

[37] Ibid., p. 4.

[38] Ibid., p. 5.

[39] Ibid., p. 6.

[40] Ibid., p. 7 (emphasis in original).

She now works with pro-life organizations and began one of her own, *And Then There Were None*, a ministry outreach offering financial, emotional, spiritual, and legal support for anyone who wants to leave the abortion industry. In its first six months, the group's website reported thirty-four abortion clinic workers walking out and contacting them for help.

> At one point, we had three workers from one clinic. Exoduses like this absolutely cripple abortion facilities....
>
> There are about 650 abortion clinics in the country. If we estimate an average of about five employees per facility, we can assume there are currently about 3,300 abortion clinic employees in the United States....
>
> We are currently working with two abortionists.... Abortion workers are leaving, and they are taking their friends with them. These FORMER workers are now reaching into the same clinics where they once worked. They are sharing their new found joy with their friends still trapped in the industry.[41]

Pregnancy help centers are proliferating across the country, usually in close proximity to abortion clinics. They offer women in crisis pregnancies all the help and support they may need, throughout the pregnancy and after the baby's birth, as an alternative to abortion. So there really is a choice.

## Let's Be Clear:

1. *Every* innocent person has the right to life. *Nobody* has the right to take that life. "Human life must be respected and protected absolutely from the moment of conception. From the first moment of his existence, a human being must be recognized as having the rights of a person—among which is the inviolable right of every innocent being to life."[42] This is an innate right. No person or government has the right to take this away.
2. The child in the womb is a separate innocent person in his most vulnerable form. Therefore, every child in the womb has the right to life, and nobody has the right to take it.

[41] Abby Johnson, "The 1%", And Then There Were None, Oct. 29, 2012, http://archive.aweber.com/attwn/KDNbM/t/The_1_.htm.

[42] *Catechism of the Catholic Church*, no. 2270.

3. **Abortion (i.e., the killing of the child in the womb) kills an existing human being.** Before becoming Pope Francis, Archbishop Jorge Bergoglio stated:

> The moral problem with abortion is of a pre-religious nature because the genetic code of the person is present at the moment of conception. There is already a human being. . . . To not allow further progress in the development of a being that already has the entire genetic code of a human being is not ethical. The right to life is the first human right. Abortion is killing someone that cannot defend himself.[43]

4. **The right to life is a basic right. All other rights are based on this one.** Pope John Paul II declared:

> It is impossible to further the common good without acknowledging and defending the right to life, upon which all the other inalienable rights of individuals are founded and from which they develop. A society lacks solid foundations when, on the one hand, it asserts values such as the dignity of the person, justice and peace, but then, on the other hand, radically acts to the contrary by allowing or tolerating a variety of ways in which human life is devalued and violated, especially where it is weak or marginalized.[44]

5. **Even though abortion may be legal, it remains immoral.**

> If you've got an immoral law, you've got to work to change that. You've got children being killed every day. It goes on forever. That's the great scandal, and that's why there's such a sense of urgency now. There's no recognition of the fact that children continue to be killed, and we live, therefore, in a country drenched in blood. This can't be something that you start playing off pragmatically against other issues.[45]

[43] Jorge Mario Bergoglio and Abraham Skorka, *On Heaven and Earth: Pope Francis on Faith, Family and the Church in the 21st Century* (New York: Image, 2013), p. 107.

[44] Pope John Paul II, *Evangelium Vitae* (Mar. 25, 1995), no. 101, http://www.vatican.va/holy_father/john_paul_ii/encyclicals/documents/hf_jp-ii_enc_25031995_evangelium-vitae_en.html.

[45] Allen, "Interview with Cardinal George".

# *Chapter 3*

# Dignity without End: Aging, Vulnerability, and Death

*In the past, great respect was shown to the elderly.... And what of today? If we stop to consider the current situation, we see that among some peoples old age is esteemed and valued, while among others this is much less the case, due to a mentality which gives priority to immediate human usefulness and productivity. Such an attitude frequently leads to contempt for the later years of life, while older people themselves are led to wonder whether their lives are still worthwhile. It has come to the point where euthanasia is increasingly put forward as a solution for difficult situations. Unfortunately, in recent years the idea of euthanasia has lost for many people the sense of horror which it naturally awakens in those who have a sense of respect for life. Certainly it can happen that, when grave illness involves unbearable suffering, the sick are tempted to despair and their loved ones or those responsible for their care feel compelled by a misguided compassion to consider the solution of "an easy death" as something reasonable.... Regardless of intentions and circumstances, euthanasia is always an intrinsically evil act, a violation of God's law and an offence against the dignity of the human person.*[1]

—Pope John Paul II

*Why now, when for the first time in human history the pain and discomforting symptoms of serious illness can be substantially alleviated, do so many find mercy killing and suicide so appealing? Think of it as a symptom rather than a cause. The euthanasia movement reflects a profound nihilism that has been spreading like a cancer throughout the West for the past hundred years.*[2]

—Wesley J. Smith, Bioethicist

[1] Pope John Paul II, *Letter to the Elderly* (Oct. 1, 1999), no. 9.

[2] Wesley J. Smith, "Assisted Suicide: The Wind in Their Sails", *First Things*, Nov. 10, 2008, http://www.firstthings.com/onthesquare/2008/11/assisted-suicide-the-wind-in-t.

*Schindler v. Schiavo* was the *Roe v. Wade* of the euthanasia movement. Terri Schiavo was as lively and healthy as most twenty-six-year-olds on the night of February 25, 1990. For reasons never determined medically or legally, she collapsed in her home, and oxygen to her brain was cut off long enough to leave her cognitively impaired. Her husband, Michael, was the only person present, and he was the one given legal guardianship over Terri without her parents' knowledge.

She recovered some cognitive abilities in therapy over the next year until Michael stopped them all. Within three years, he cut off communication with her family and their access to her, began living with another woman, refused to legally end his marriage to Terri, and fathered two children with his live-in girlfriend.

In 1995, he hired an infamous right-to-die litigator, who sought legally to remove her life support. After years of battles in court, Michael Schiavo claimed in 2000 that Terri once told him she would not want life support if ever in a condition requiring it, and he convinced Judge George Greer to order her feeding tube removed.

The long dying and death of Terri Schiavo by court-ordered starvation and dehydration was an eruption on the landscape of America. Her saga went on for many years under public radar, but it burst on the scene while she and her family were helplessly at the mercy of a legal system that had no mercy.

Major media paid attention when Congress intervened, and even, ultimately, President George W. Bush, to protect the constitutional rights of due process of an American citizen against judicial tyranny. This was a precedent setter for end-of-life law, just as Norma McCorvey served a similar purpose for the abortion movement. Only, Terri unknowingly wound up as the center of attention.

It was the beginning of the change in how we think about dying and life.

Someone in the Netherlands issued a "Letter to America" during Terri's ordeal, warning that if this country allowed this woman to die in this way, Dutch euthanasia would soon come to America. Terri Schiavo's agonizing and very public execution has become America's story in the present, as Terri's brother, Bobby Schindler, tells it.

> As hideous as it was, the truth is, long before Terri's case made headlines, the removal of basic care—food and water—was becoming commonplace. It continues to happen every day across our country oftentimes

> in cases, like Terri's, where the patient does not suffer from any life-threatening condition.
>
> Much of the problem that exists stems from a blind acceptance of misinformation that has moved us from a firm belief in the sanctity of life to a "quality of life" mindset, which says that some lives are not worth living....
>
> This shift, what I call lethal bigotry, began with the medical community, has infiltrated our judiciary and is taking over our nation. People are making decisions in place of God....
>
> The sad fact is we have become a nation that spends billions trying to find the perfect body, while ignoring the condition of our collective soul; where altruism seems to be a thing of the past, and moral relativism has become a bona fide religion.[3]

What did we learn from this? When it comes to news, people learn what they're told by the media, and the media kept distorting this story. So public polls on "what to do about Terri Schiavo" were determined by the way the questions were asked. There were limits on the public's willingness to tolerate outright euthanasia, so news stories used euphemisms to report the story on whether her family should "let her go", though she wasn't going anywhere. She was in no medical danger of death.

Terri Schiavo was profoundly brain damaged (although just how profoundly remains unknown), but she was not in a coma or on a respirator. She was not being kept alive by artificial means, any more than small children are kept alive by artificial means when their parents feed them. She had devoted parents and siblings who were willing to care for her. She could easily have gone on in these conditions for many years. She was not close to dying. For death to arrive, she would have to be killed.

> And for that to happen, the use of words like "starvation" and "dehydration" would have to be discouraged. Those words might, after all, have reminded us that what was done to Schiavo would be criminal if done to an animal and provoke cries of "torture" and "cruel and unusual punishment" if done to a convicted capital murderer. And "killed," of course, was totally verboten. Schiavo was being "removed from life support," not denied basic sustenance.[4]

[3] Bobby Schindler, "The Dehydration Death of a Nation", *World Net Daily Commentary*, Mar. 30, 2007, http://www.wnd.com/2007/03/40848/.

[4] "Killed by Euphemisms", editorial, *National Review Online*, Mar. 31, 2005, http://www.nationalreview.com/articles/214051/killed-euphemisms/editors.

Furthermore ... "The phrase 'persistent vegetative state' had to be repeated constantly, never mind that basic tests were never performed to establish this diagnosis, and such diagnoses have a very high error rate, and treated as though it meant 'brain death'."[5]

That set the bar for a new and insidious diagnosis.

## Life Unworthy of Life

News coverage of Terri Schiavo certainly included or favored the meme that her "choice to die" was being "honored", although, as the *National Review Online* pointed out,

> the evidence that she had, at age 26, given any considered thought to her own mortality and potential incapacity was thin and highly suspect—its lone source being a husband who incongruously proclaimed his solemn fidelity to this purported wish of Terri even as he started up a new family, denied Terri basic care, and insisted on denying her heartbroken parents their desire to care for their child.
>
> The charade here was not performed to protect Terri Schiavo's dignity but to increase the public's comfort with the devaluation of life. So it was that Michael Schiavo's lawyer, the euthanasia enthusiast George Felos, sketched for the media (which was naturally not permitted to observe Terri's deteriorating condition) a rosy portrait of Terri's extremis: radiantly beautiful, soothed by soft music and the comfort of a stuffed animal....
>
> The scene, of course, was not set for her. By Felos's account, she was just an insensate, post-human corpse, for whom such tender touches were irrelevant—the comforts that would have made a difference, food and water, having been mercilessly denied. This was theater for the American people.[6]

And you don't know what you're not told.

> Why not kill Mrs. Schiavo quickly and efficiently, by depriving her of air to breathe? In principle, that would have been no different from denying her the other basic necessities of life. Why not give her a lethal injection? The law would not have allowed those methods; but the reason nobody advocated them was that they would have been too obviously murder. So the court-ordered killing was carried out slowly, incrementally, over

[5] Ibid.

[6] Ibid.

> days and weeks, with soft music, stuffed animals, and euphonious slogans about choice and dignity and radiance. By the time it ended, no one really remembered how many days and hours it had gone on. The nation accepted it, national polls supported it, and we all moved on to other things.[7]

Painfully true. Here's one of the consequences:

> Next time it will be easier. It always is. The tolerance of early-term abortion made it possible to tolerate partial-birth abortion, and to give advanced thinkers a hearing when they advocate outright infanticide. Letting the courts decide such life-and-death issues made it possible for us to let them decide others, made it seem somehow wrong for anyone to stand in their way. Now they are helping to snuff out the minimally conscious. Who's next?[8]

Princeton Professor Robert P. George served on George W. Bush's President's Council on Bioethics at the time. He considered the gravity of this case in an interview with the *National Review Online*.

> What we must avoid, always and everywhere, is yielding to the temptation to regard some human lives, or the lives of human beings in certain conditions, as *lebensunwerten Lebens*, lives unworthy of life. Since the life of every human being has inherent worth and dignity, there is no valid category of *lebensunwerten Lebens*. Any society that supposes that there is such a category has deeply morally compromised itself. As Leon Kass recently reminded us in a powerful address at the Holocaust Museum, it was supposedly enlightened and progressive German academics and medical people who put their nation on the road to shame more than a decade before the Nazis rose to power by promoting a doctrine of eugenics based precisely on the proposition that the lives of some human beings—such as the severely retarded—are unworthy of life.[9]

The well-known Nazi Holocaust was preceded by a lesser-known extermination project carried out on large numbers of vulnerable, disabled, and impaired patients. Dr. Mark Mostert of Human Life Matters exposed Hitler's insidious Aktion T-4 program in a Regent University

[7] Ibid.

[8] Ibid.

[9] "Always to Care, Never to Kill: Terri Schiavo and the Right to Life", interview, *National Review Online*, Mar. 21, 2005, http://www.nationalreview.com/articles/213958/always-care-never-kill-interview.

paper called "Useless Eaters: Disability as Genocidal Marker in Nazi Germany".[10] The "useless eaters" idea carries considerable currency in evolving standards for treating disabled and impaired patients here and now, especially with health care rationing increasing, as the California Medical Association editorial predicted it would—by necessity, editors claimed—in 1970.

The idea of treating certain classes of people as less worthy or unworthy of rights is too harsh in those terms, so the ideas of eugenics had to be parsed out and sold to the public separately under the mantle of "rights".

The goal of the "right-to-die" movement was to market the idea better. The "Hemlock Society" became "Compassion and Choices". "Physician-assisted suicide" became "aid in dying". The natural inclination to protect and save lives used to be a fundamental characteristic of our society. One hopes it still is for most people. But it is changing, and we must be aware of the ways those changes are seeping into the culture and our institutions.

The *Magazine* of the *New York Times* devoted a lengthy look at this in a 2008 story titled "The Urge to End It All". It opened with a reality check.

> "There is but one truly serious philosophical problem," Albert Camus wrote, "and that is suicide." How to explain why, among the only species capable of pondering its own demise, whose desperate attempts to forestall mortality have spawned both armies and branches of medicine in a perpetual search for the Fountain of Youth, there are those who, by their own hand, would choose death over life? Our contradictory reactions to the act speak to the conflicted hold it has on our imaginations: revulsion mixed with fascination, scorn leavened with pity. It is a cardinal sin—but change the packaging a little, and suicide assumes the guise of heroism or high passion, the stuff of literature and art.[11]

Social engineers have changed the packaging a lot, and public reactions have followed.

> Little wonder, then, that most of us have come to regard suicide with an element of resignation, even as a particularly brutal form of social

[10] Mark P. Mostert, "Useless Eaters: Disability as Genocidal Marker in Nazi Germany", *Journal of Special Education* 36, no. 3 (2002): 155–68.

[11] Scott Anderson, "The Urge to End It All", *New York Times Magazine*, July 6, 2008, http://www.nytimes.com/2008/07/06/magazine/06suicide-t.html.

> Darwinism: perhaps through luck or medication or family intervention some suicidal individuals can be identified and saved, but in the larger scheme of things, there will always be those driven to take their own lives, and there's really not much that we can do about it.[12]

That was in 2008. Now "aid in dying" has become a "rights" cause, and family intervention is sliding more now to the aid of helping someone go through with it out of the tortured logic that it is compassionate.

The "right-to-die" or "aid in dying" movement was behind new guidelines spreading through the states on how to administer (or withhold) life-sustaining treatment for patients needing palliative care. In over half the states, some version of orders to end life-sustaining treatment is in place. People either don't know these changes are happening, don't understand what they mean when they do hear about them, or are left frightened and confused when they face comfort care choices or end-of-life decisions about their own loved ones, which most of us inevitably do.

Dr. Elizabeth Wickham, cofounder and executive director of the Life Tree Christian educational ministry, published a thorough and documented warning in *Celebrate Life* magazine explaining the terms, their origin, and trajectory. "Traditional palliative care was symptom management", she wrote. "Today's palliative care involves a palliative care team (which can include physicians, nurses, social workers, and chaplains) that helps the family determine when the patient's care should be shifted away from cure and toward death."[13] How does the team determine that? They follow guidelines developed by a task force with these recurring themes:

- "Everyone should have an advance directive to protect himself from unnecessary medical treatment at the end of life."
- "Withholding or withdrawing food and water is a natural—and even pleasant—way to die and a perfectly ethical means of controlling the time of death."
- "The principle of double effect in the use of pain treatment justifies terminal (palliative) sedation."[14]

[12] Ibid.

[13] Elizabeth D. Wickham, Ph.D., "Today's 'Palliative Care' Disrespects the Natural Law", *Celebrate Life*, Sept./Oct. 2012, http://www.clmagazine.org/article/index/id/MTA5NjE.

[14] Ibid.

Any Catholic who understands the Church's social moral teaching can see the red flags in these.

## Patient's Rights/Human Rights

Take Wisconsin, for example, as a microcosm of the morphing healthcare system redefining health and care. Milwaukee Archbishop Jerome Listecki's letter to the president of a Wisconsin hospital in his diocese in late 2011 is revealing:

> In this ongoing changing world, healthcare providers are constantly challenged by ideology, procedures and issues that hide or disguise the dignity of human life. We turn our eyes to Christ who reveals to us the true meaning of life and human dignity.
>
> It is in that regard that I write to you today about the moral concerns regarding the use of Physician Orders for Life-Sustaining Treatment (POLST). After carefully studying the POLST form and paradigm and consulting our Archdiocesan Healthcare and Bioethics Committee, I have confirmed my serious reservations regarding the use of POLST.[15]

Within months, the Wisconsin bishops collectively released a statement warning people about the spreading use of POLST. They did it in a carefully but clearly worded pastoral letter, *Upholding the Dignity of Human Life.*

> A POLST form presents options for treatments as if they were morally neutral. In fact, they are not. Because we cannot predict the future, it is difficult to determine in advance whether specific medical treatments, from an ethical perspective, are absolutely necessary or optional. These decisions depend upon factors such as the benefits, expected outcomes, and the risks or burdens of the treatment.
>
> A POLST oversimplifies these decisions and bears the real risk that an indication may be made on it to withhold a treatment that, in particular circumstances, might be an act of euthanasia. Despite the possible benefits of these documents, this risk is too grave to be acceptable.
>
> Finally, the design and use of the POLST document raises concerns as to whether it accurately reflects and protects a person's wishes....
>
> ... We encourage all persons to use a durable power of attorney for health care. For those who are age 18 or older, completing this document

[15] Archbishop Jerome E. Listecki, Letter to Andrew J. Bagnall, President and Chief Executive Officer of St. Nicholas Hospital in Sheboygan, Wisconsin, Nov. 2, 2011.

> allows you to appoint a trusted person to make health care decisions on your behalf if a situation arises in which you cannot make these decisions for yourself. It is important to discuss your wishes and Catholic teaching with the person whom you appoint and to choose someone who will make health care decisions based on these principles.[16]

The bishops' recommendation for a durable power of attorney, essentially, is the moral, ethical, and safe alternative to a "living will". Some call this alternative a "will to live" document, but the Patients' Rights Council calls it a Protective Medical Decisions Document (PMDD) and provides them online.[17]

> It gives the person you name to make your health care decisions the authority to act on your behalf. That person is generally referred to as your "agent."
>
> The PMDD limits your agent's authority in one specific way. It clearly states that your agent does not have the authority to approve the *direct and intentional* ending of your life.
>
> For example, your agent may not authorize that you be given a lethal injection or an intentional drug overdose. Further, your agent may not direct that you be denied food or fluids *for the purpose of causing your death* by starvation or dehydration.
>
> This limitation not only protects you, but it also protects your agent from being subjected to pressure to authorize such actions.
>
> The PMDD also has specific directions that are necessary in the current medical climate.
>
> For example, some health care providers have taken it upon themselves to put Do Not Resuscitate (DNR) orders in place without the patient's or agent's authorization. Similarly, some health care providers, ethics committees and health facilities are making decisions about what is "appropriate" or "beneficial" based on institutional cost-containment considerations, not on the basis of what is best for or wanted by the patient.[18]

[16] Wisconsin Catholic Conference, *Upholding the Dignity of Human Life: A Pastoral Statement on Physician Orders for Life-Sustaining Treatment (POLST) from the Catholic Bishops of Wisconsin* (July 2012), http://www.wisconsincatholic.org/WCC%20Upholding%20Dignity%20POLST%20Statement%20FINAL%207-23.pdf.

[17] See the Patients' Rights Council website for more information: http://www.patientsrightscouncil.org/site/do-you-need-an-advance-directive/.

[18] Patients' Rights Council, "Advance Directives: Do You Need an Advance Directive?" (2013), http://www.patientsrightscouncil.org/site/do-you-need-an-advance-directive (emphasis in original).

The Terri Schiavo ordeal launched the national debate in media, and around many kitchen tables when families started hearing they needed a "living will" to avoid someone pulling the plug on them, or to assure that their wishes would be honored if they wound up in a debilitated state in a medical center. But what they weren't hearing much about is the danger of standard "living wills" nor about these safer alternatives.

The Vatican is well aware of this evolving health care debate and threat to innocent human lives, and it has issued statements and clarifications reaffirming Church teaching. One such is this key response to U.S. bishops' questions on the ethical imperatives of providing nutrition and hydration.

> **First question:** *Is the administration of food and water (whether by natural or artificial means) to a patient in a "vegetative state" morally obligatory except when they cannot be assimilated by the patient's body or cannot be administered to the patient without causing significant physical discomfort?*
>
> **Response:** Yes. The administration of food and water even by artificial means is, in principle, an ordinary and proportionate means of preserving life. It is therefore obligatory to the extent to which, and for as long as, it is shown to accomplish its proper finality, which is the hydration and nourishment of the patient. In this way, suffering and death by starvation and dehydration are prevented.
>
> **Second question:** *When nutrition and hydration are being supplied by artificial means to a patient in a "permanent vegetative state", may they be discontinued when competent physicians judge with moral certainty that the patient will never recover consciousness?*
>
> **Response:** No. A patient in a "permanent vegetative state" is a person with fundamental human dignity and must, therefore, receive ordinary and proportionate care which includes, in principle, the administration of water and food even by artificial means.[19]

In fact, Pope John Paul II took exception to the medical terms applied to human persons in his March 2004 address to the participants in the

[19] Congregation for the Doctrine of the Faith, "Responses to Certain Questions of the United States Conference of Catholic Bishops concerning Artificial Nutrition and Hydration" (Aug. 1, 2007), http://www.vatican.va/roman_curia/congregations/cfaith/documents/rc_con_cfaith_doc_20070801_risposte-usa_en.html.

international congress on "Life-Sustaining Treatments and Vegetative State: Scientific Advances and Ethical Dilemmas".

> [T]he term *permanent vegetative state* has been coined to indicate the condition of those patients whose "vegetative state" continues for over a year. Actually, there is no different diagnosis that corresponds to such a definition, but only a conventional prognostic judgment, relative to the fact that the recovery of patients, statistically speaking, is ever more difficult as the condition of vegetative state is prolonged in time.
>
> However, we must neither forget nor underestimate that there are well-documented cases of at least partial recovery even after many years; *we can thus state that medical science, up until now, is still unable to predict with certainty who among patients in this condition will recover and who will not* [my italics].
>
> ... Faced with patients in similar clinical conditions, there are some who cast doubt on the persistence of the "human quality" itself, *almost as if the adjective "vegetative" (whose use is now solidly established), which symbolically describes a clinical state, could or should be instead applied to the sick as such, actually demeaning their value and personal dignity* [my italics]....
>
> In opposition to such trends of thought, I feel the duty to reaffirm strongly that the intrinsic value and personal dignity of every human being do not change, no matter what the concrete circumstances of his or her life. *A man, even if seriously ill or disabled in the exercise of his highest functions, is and always will be a man*, and he will never become a "vegetable" or an "animal"....
>
> The sick person in a vegetative state, awaiting recovery or a natural end, still has the right to basic health care (nutrition, hydration, cleanliness, warmth, etc.), and to the prevention of complications related to his confinement to bed. He also has the right to appropriate rehabilitative care and to be monitored for clinical signs of eventual recovery.
>
> I should like particularly to underline how the administration of water and food, even when provided by artificial means, always represents a *natural means* of preserving life, not a *medical act*. Its use, furthermore, should be considered, in principle, *ordinary* and *proportionate*, and as such morally obligatory, insofar as and until it is seen to have attained its proper finality, which in the present case consists in providing nourishment to the patient and alleviation of his suffering.[20]

[20] Pope John Paul II, "Address of John Paul II to the Participants in the International Congress on 'Life-Sustaining Treatments and Vegetative State: Scientific Advances and Ethical Dilemmas'" (Mar. 20, 2004), nos. 2–3, http://www.vatican.va/holy_father/john_paul_ii/speeches/2004/march/documents/hf_jp-ii_spe_20040320_congress-fiamc_en.html (emphasis in original).

But he went further . . .

> However, it is not enough to reaffirm the general principle according to which the value of a man's life cannot be made subordinate to any judgment of its quality expressed by other men; it is necessary to promote the *taking of positive actions* as a stand against pressures to withdraw hydration and nutrition as a way to put an end to the lives of these patients.
>
> It is necessary, above all, to *support those families* who have had one of their loved ones struck down by this terrible clinical condition. They cannot be left alone with their heavy human, psychological and financial burden. Although the care for these patients is not, in general, particularly costly, society must allot sufficient resources for the care of this sort of frailty, by way of bringing about appropriate, concrete initiatives.[21]

These are critical distinctions. Learning and grasping them have become urgent tasks with rapidly changing medical technology, health care law, and prevailing cultural attitudes. The Church continues to engage biomedical issues as swiftly as they advance and, in the process, help Catholics make moral, ethical, and humane decisions.

## Embryonic Stem Cell Research and Cloning

This issue seems to be out of the news and therefore far out on the horizon. Not so for long. It was a hot-button issue in the 2006 U.S. elections, with Hollywood celebrities advocating for passage of Missouri's ballot initiative to allow funding for embryonic stem cell research. Voters narrowly passed it.

It was false science to claim that destructive human embryonic stem cell research promised medical breakthroughs in cures when it was proven only to be unsuccessful and even threatening (sometimes producing tumors) while other, ethical stem cell research progressed with huge successes.

Adult stem cell research, the uncontroversial, moral stem cell science, has advanced over the years and offers the most promising treatment for a range of serious medical conditions. But the biotechnology industry sank a lot of money into embryonic stem cell research, promising it was only for treatment (though unsuccessful) and not reproduction (widely resisted by a somewhat anchored public). So it's only a matter of time before they announce the creation of the first human cloned embryo,

[21] Ibid.

and then justify the existence of this cloned human to produce many more for scientific research.

Bioethics expert Wesley J. Smith, who writes a column under the heading "Human Exceptionalism", predicts this is coming.

> When—not if—that happens, the heated public debate will make the ESCR [embryonic stem cell research] brouhaha seem like a day at Disneyland.
>
> Proponents of human cloning believe it offers tremendous scientific potential and the opportunity to make fortunes. But opponents like myself—both on the political left and right—strongly believe that human cloning is intrinsically immoral, meaning that no potential utilitarian benefit justifies developing the technology.[22]

All sorts of inhumane possibilities are tied up in this futuristic pursuit, and he reviews several. But this line chills: "Cloning is also *the* essential technology to learning how to genetically engineer human life, a technology with which 'transhumanists' hope to create a 'post-human species'."[23] Even the U.N. General Assembly urged support for an international treaty outlawing all human cloning.[24] "We can—and should—pursue ethical biotechnological research to treat disease and improve the human condition without concomitantly infringing on the intrinsic value of human life."[25]

But we need a common understanding of the definition and value of human life. At the highest levels of power and influence, there are some glaring examples of misunderstanding of the very nature (or fundamental facts) of human life.

In March 2009, former president Bill Clinton talked with CNN's Dr. Sanjay Gupta about the moral difference between using embryos for research that have even a remote possibility of being fertilized ... and other embryos. This left the viewer agape, given what they should have both known of the facts of human biology—such as the fact that an embryo only exists because of fertilization.

[22] Wesley J. Smith, "The Coming Public Conflict over Human Cloning", *First Things*, Jan. 11, 2013, http://www.firstthings.com/onthesquare/2013/01/the-coming-public-conflict-over-human-cloning.

[23] Ibid.

[24] United Nations, "General Assembly Adopts United Nations Declaration on Human Cloning by Vote of 84-34-37", United Nations Press Release GA/10333, 2005, http://www.un.org/News/Press/docs/2005/ga10333.doc.htm.

[25] Smith, "Coming Public Conflict".

Clinton uses this language over and over, and Gupta does nothing to correct the terminology or the discussion. In fact, he seems to agree, which is concerning since Gupta is a medical doctor and one whom President Obama considered appointing as Surgeon General. And yet, Gupta refers to Clinton as someone "who studied this", thus giving him deference on the topic. Gupta asks if this controversial issue will remain this divisive and "be the abortion of the next generation?"[26] (revealing that he, Dr. Gupta, is unaware or in denial of the fact that harvesting stem cells from embryos *de facto* destroys that human being's developing life).

Here's Clinton's response: "If it's obvious that we're not taking embryos that can—that under any conceivable scenario would be used for a process that would allow them to be fertilized and become little babies, and I think if it's obvious that we're not talking about some science fiction cloning of human beings, then I think the American people will support this."[27] Clarification is needed here, though it seems self-evident. Embryos already are fertilized, and are already little (the smallest) human babies.

Gupta asks if he has "any reservations?" Clinton responds:

> I don't know that I have any reservations, but I was—he [President Obama] has apparently decided to leave to the relevant professional committees the definition of which frozen embryos are basically going to be discarded, because they're not going to be fertilized. I believe the American people believe it's a pro-life decision to use an embryo that's frozen and never going to be fertilized for embryonic stem cell research, especially since now, not withstanding some promising developments, most of the scientists in this field and the doctors will tell you they don't know of any other source as good as embryonic stem cells for all the various things that need to be researched.[28]

This is an absolutely stunning set of statements winding up in a complete untruth. But there's more ...

> But those committees need to be really careful to make sure if they don't want a big storm to be stirred up here, that any of the embryos that are

[26] "Bill Clinton on Health Care Reform", *CNN Larry King Live*, transcript, Mar. 11, 2009, http://edition.cnn.com/TRANSCRIPTS/0903/11/lkl.01.html.

[27] Ibid.

[28] Ibid.

used clearly have been placed beyond the pale of being fertilized before their use. There are a large number of embryos that we know are never going to be fertilized, where the people who are in control of them have made that clear. The research ought to be confined to those.[29]

Mr. Clinton did say this, and Dr. Gupta did not clarify the biological and scientific facts.

Clinton continues: "But there are values involved that we all ought to feel free to discuss in all scientific research. And that is the one thing that I think these committees need to make it clear that they're not going to fool with any embryos where there's any possibility, even if it's somewhat remote, that they could be fertilized and become human beings."[30]

This glaring misstatement and misinformed thought process has grave consequences. Many women who go into abortion clinics out of desperation or under pressure do not realize that the baby—the unique, separate, individual human being she conceived—is already in their womb. Perhaps it's even the majority who think that. They think (and often hear repeated by abortion clinic workers) that it's a blob of tissue at that stage, and abortion will prevent that child from coming into existence. So they go ahead with it (which is why the abortion movement so fiercely resists "informed consent" laws) and later suffer the trauma of post-abortion syndrome when they come to learn or understand that abortion took the lives of their children.

And here are some of the highest members of government and media perpetuating the misinformation.

In December 2010, Fox News host Bill O'Reilly discussed with former Fox contributor Margaret Hoover the story of a couple conducting a poll on their blog about whether or not the wife should have an abortion. Here's a snip from the transcript:

Bill O'Reilly, Host: [A thirty-year old woman], 19 weeks pregnant, is thinking about terminating her fetus because she's in a bad emotional state, according to her blog. [Her husband] disputes some of this. But there is no disputing the fact the couple has asked Americans to vote on whether the abortion should take place, and two million people have....

[29] Ibid.
[30] Ibid.

> No. 1, this is disgusting. This is a human life we're talking about, is it not?
>
> MARGARET HOOVER, FOX NEWS ANALYST: This is a potential human life.
>
> O'REILLY: I don't mind your description there. It's a potential human being containing human DNA right at this moment.
>
> HOOVER: Correct.[31]

He was right when he first stated the central debate was over a human life. And wrong when he backpedaled.

> O'REILLY: So it's disgusting that you would put this up for a vote on whether to execute it. Am I wrong?
>
> HOOVER: The decision to have an abortion is a deeply personal decision between a woman, her family, her doctor, her God; not her government, and not the public at large.
>
> O'REILLY: OK. So you're with me on that.[32]

Not really, as it turned out. It seemed that Bill O'Reilly was trying to find common ground to gain some currency with Ms. Hoover in the larger argument that the decision about terminating nascent human life is not open for public debate or polling.

But Mr. O'Reilly declares himself to be pro-life, and yet he used the language of the abortion movement by saying a woman who is nineteen weeks pregnant is "thinking about terminating her fetus".

Mr. O'Reilly is very intelligent. He usually tries to keep arguments grounded in facts and not hypotheses or speculation or euphemism or political agenda. So he should have known that statement plays into the abortion argument, one which has inflicted tremendous pain and trauma on post-abortive women and, frankly, death on their children in the womb.

[31] "Couple Conducting Poll on Their Blog about Whether or Not They Should Have an Abortion", *The O'Reilly Factor*, Fox News, transcript, Dec. 2, 2010, http://www.foxnews.com/on-air/oreilly/transcript/couple-conducting-poll-their-blog-about-whether-not-they-should-have-abortion.

[32] Ibid.

## Moral Obligations at the End of Life

How we think about these issues that involve the end of human life derive from how we regard the sanctity and dignity of all human life. The false premise at the center of the "right to die" movement is that it upholds the very progressive ideal of radical personal autonomy. That is another marketing ploy.

In 2010, a self-proclaimed atheistic "radical humanist" challenged the premise and the whole movement. An online forum for "free-thinkers", called *Spiked*, published the speech that editor Brendan O'Neill gave to the South Place Ethical Society in London in 2010 to debate assisted dying with "Dignity in Dying", "Care Not Killing", and other groups. Here is what he said in part:

> For me, one of the great mysteries of modern times is how the "right to die" came to be seen as an important progressive cause.
>
> It has now reached a level where if you tell someone that you have liberal instincts, humanist tendencies, and you don't follow any religious faith, they will automatically assume that you are in favour of legalising assisted suicide. There is almost an unspoken, nudge-nudge agreement amongst a certain section of society that this is a just and righteous campaign ... you support assisted dying.
>
> As a result, when I tell people that I am deeply uncomfortable with the campaign for the "right to die", and I am not convinced that assisted dying should be legalised, they give me funny looks. They instantly assume that I must be one of "Them"—one of those religious people, one of those strange individuals who thinks human life is so sacred that no one should ever be allowed to die until God wants them to.
>
> But I'm not. I'm an atheist. And I consider myself a radical humanist. However, I am also very worried about the drive to legalise assisted dying. I think we need to start making the *humanist* case against this fashion for voluntary euthanasia.
>
> There are two reasons why, as someone driven by a human-centred morality, I am uncomfortable with legalising assisted dying. Firstly, because it will be bad for the people it is supposed to help: terminally ill people who want to die. And secondly, because it will also be bad for those people who want to live, people who might be sick or disabled or old but who want to continue living.[33]

[33] Brendan O'Neill, "The Humanist Case against Euthanasia", *Spiked Online*, May 17, 2010, http://www.spiked-online.com/index.php/site/article/8887.

One example is Rom Houben, the man who came out of a twenty-three-year-long coma to tell the horrors of being unable to tell doctors he was conscious.

> "I screamed, but there was nothing to hear," said Mr Houben ... who doctors thought was in a persistent vegetative state. "I dreamed myself away," he added, tapping his tale out with the aid of a computer....
>
> Mr Houben said: "All that time I just literally dreamed of a better life. Frustration is too small a word to describe what I felt."
>
> His case [was] ... revealed in a scientific paper released by the man who "saved" him, top neurological expert Dr Steven Laureys.
>
> "Medical advances caught up with him," said Dr Laureys, who believes there may be many similar cases of false comas around the world. The disclosure will also renew the right-to-die debate over whether people in comas are truly unconscious.[34]

Does the brain create the mind? That's only one of the countless questions raised by the wrenching Terri Schiavo ordeal that riveted the world and has continued to have repercussions in all sorts of debates. The ramifications of that pivotal event are only getting broader and deeper.

A Yale neurologist and a fellow neurosurgeon carried on a published debate in 2008 over the handling of the Terri Schiavo ordeal. The neurosurgeon, Dr. Michael Egnor, wrote this in a commentary for an online news site.

> "Persistent vegetative state," defined succinctly but accurately, is the denial of subjective experience in a brain-damaged human being. PVS is the medical assertion that a human being is an object, but not a subject.
>
> PVS is the only modern medical diagnosis that denies the personhood of a patient, and thus is fraught with logical and ethical problems.
>
> Furthermore, patients diagnosed with PVS are precisely those patients in whom discernment of awareness is most unreliable.
>
> We can never directly apprehend the thoughts of other people; we infer the thoughts of others only by their behavior. Patients with severe brain damage are precisely those people in whom expression of behavior is most impaired and in whom diagnoses based on assessment of behavior are most unreliable.[35]

[34] Allan Hall, "'I Screamed, But There Was Nothing to Hear': Man Trapped in 23-year 'Coma' Reveals Horror of Being Unable to Tell Doctors He was Conscious", *Daily Mail Online*, Nov. 23, 2009, http://www.dailymail.co.uk/news/article-1230092/Rom-Houben-Patient-trapped-23-year-coma-conscious-along.html#axzz2K4lgTW7N.

[35] Dr. Michael Egnor, "Terri Schiavo's Death and the Misdiagnosis of a Persistent Vegetative State", *Lifenews.com*, Aug. 12, 2008, http://archive.lifenews.com/bio2544.html.

So we get the "materialist" reaction to consider these patients "objects but not subjects", making it easier to stop caring for them as if they were persons. "In my view, the political efforts to save Ms. Schiavo's life were well-intentioned and completely justified. I believe that many of the medical opinions offered publicly by physicians who favored withdrawal of Ms. Schiavo's hydration and nourishment were rank pseudoscience. What was done to Ms. Schiavo was an atrocity."[36]

We have guides through this dangerous new frontier. The *Manhattan Declaration* sums up the resolve of its movement:

> A truly prophetic Christian witness will insistently call on those who have been entrusted with temporal power to fulfill the first responsibility of government: to protect the weak and vulnerable against violent attack, and to do so with no favoritism, partiality, or discrimination. The Bible enjoins us to defend those who cannot defend themselves, to speak for those who cannot themselves speak. And so we defend and speak for the unborn, the disabled, and the dependent. What the Bible and the light of reason make clear, we must make clear. We must be willing to defend, even at risk and cost to ourselves and our institutions, the lives of our brothers and sisters at every stage of development and in every condition.[37]

The U.S. bishops' document *Forming Consciences for Faithful Citizenship* sums up the Church's clear teaching:

> The consistent ethic of life ... anchors the Catholic commitment to defend human life, from conception until natural death, in the fundamental moral obligation to respect the dignity of every person as a child of God. It unites us as a "people of life and for life" (*Evangelium Vitae*, no. 6) pledged to build what Pope John Paul II called a "culture of life" (*Evangelium Vitae*, no. 77). *This culture of life begins with the preeminent obligation to protect innocent life from direct attack and extends to defending life whenever it is threatened or diminished.*[38]

Every part of that statement is critical. It is unambiguous. So is this:

> Human life is sacred. The dignity of the human person is the foundation of a moral vision for society. Direct attacks on innocent persons are

[36] Ibid.

[37] *Manhattan Declaration: A Call of Christian Conscience* (Nov. 20, 2009), p. 4, http://manhattandeclaration.org/man_dec_resources/Manhattan_Declaration_full_text.pdf.

[38] USCCB, *Forming Consciences for Faithful Citizenship*, no. 40, http://www.usccb.org/issues-and-action/faithful-citizenship/forming-consciences-for-faithful-citizenship-part-one.cfm, (emphasis added).

> never morally acceptable, at any stage or in any condition. In our society, human life is especially under direct attack from abortion. Other direct threats to the sanctity of human life include euthanasia, human cloning, and the destruction of human embryos for research.[39]

We can never, directly or indirectly, be complicit in any of these.

"In a sensible world, none of these things would be in question", remarked Archbishop Chaput when the *Manhattan Declaration* was released. "But we no longer live in a sensible world."[40]

## Let's Be Clear:

1. **At no point does a human person lose or outgrow (by either age or condition) his innate dignity and worth.**

   > The intrinsic value and personal dignity of every human being do not change, no matter what the concrete circumstances of his or her life. *A man, even if seriously ill or disabled in the exercise of his highest functions, is and always will be a man,* and he will never become a 'vegetable' or an 'animal'. Even our brothers and sisters who find themselves in the clinical condition of a 'vegetative state' retain their human dignity in all its fullness.[41]

2. **Everyone has the right to the ordinary and proportionate means of preserving his life.** These means include nutrition, hydration, basic care for the body, and sufficient medical attention to allow for a possible recovery. As John Paul II stressed, "the administration of water and food, even when provided by artificial means, always represents a *natural means* of preserving life, not a *medical act*".[42] All involved with the care of the patient are morally obliged to administer these basic means of life support as long as those means are nourishing the patient's body and alleviating his pain.

[39] Ibid., no. 44.

[40] "Archbishop Chaput: Manhattan Declaration Will 'Galvanize' Christians in Difficult Times", *Catholic News Agency*, Dec. 7, 2009, http://www.catholicnewsagency.com/news/archbishop_chaput_manhattan_declaration_will_galvanize_christians_in_difficult_times.

[41] Pope John Paul II, "Life-Sustaining Treatments and Vegetative State", no. 3 (emphasis in original).

[42] Ibid., no. 4 (emphasis in original).

3. Hastening the end of a person's life is not compassionate; it is cruel. Even if there is no prognosis for recovery, or if the patient is judged to be in a "persistent vegetative state", it is not right to pull nutrition and hydration from a patient whose body is relying upon it for life. "Death by starvation or dehydration is, in fact, the only possible outcome as a result of their withdrawal. In this sense it ends up becoming, if done knowingly and willingly, true and proper euthanasia by omission."[43] The reason for this is that the human person, at all stages and levels of functioning, remains a creation of God worthy of life.
4. However, when life support becomes *extraordinary* or *disproportionate*, it is no longer morally obligatory. As long as a person is able to take in nutrition and hydration, and those means do not themselves become a significant source of pain, they remain ordinary and proportionate (i.e., morally obligatory) means of life support. They cease from being ordinary and proportionate when the patient's body stops assimilating them or they become a significant burden on the patient (e.g., by becoming a source of significant pain for the patient). At that point, one may morally forego the administration of nutrition and hydration. "When inevitable death is imminent in spite of the means used, it is permitted in conscience to take the decision to refuse forms of treatment that would only secure a precarious and burdensome prolongation of life, so long as the normal care due to the sick person in similar cases is not interrupted."[44]

[43] Ibid. (emphasis in original).

[44] Sacred Congregation for the Doctrine of the Faith, *Declaration on Euthanasia* (May 5, 1980), part IV, http://www.vatican.va/roman_curia/congregations/cfaith/documents/rc_con_cfaith_doc_19800505_euthanasia_en.html. Cf. United States Conference of Catholic Bishops, *Ethical and Religious Directives for Catholic Health Facilities* (1971), nos. 55–58.

# Chapter 4

# Dignity in Love: Marriage

*In marriage man and woman are so firmly united as to become—to use the words of the Book of Genesis—"one flesh" (Gen 2:24). Male and female in their physical constitution, the two human subjects, even though physically different, share equally in the capacity to live "in truth and love". This capacity, characteristic of the human being as a person, has at the same time both a spiritual and a bodily dimension. It is also through the body that man and woman are predisposed to form a "communion of persons" in marriage. When they are united by the conjugal covenant in such a way as to become "one flesh" (Gen 2:24), their union ought to take place "in truth and love", and thus express the maturity proper to persons created in the image and likeness of God.*[1]

—Pope John Paul II

*Political interest can never be separated in the long run from moral right.*[2]

—Thomas Jefferson

*Vast human experience confirms that marriage is the original and most important institution for sustaining the health, education, and welfare of all persons in a society.*[3]

—*Manhattan Declaration*

The family is the foundation of society. It has always had a "decisive role" in the "demographic, ethical, pedagogical, economic and political" good

[1] Pope John Paul II, *Gratissimam Sane*, Letter to Families from Pope John Paul II (Feb. 2, 1994), no. 8.

[2] Thomas Jefferson, Letter to James Monroe (1806), cited in Paul Leicester Ford, *The Writings of Thomas Jefferson (FE)*, vol. 8 (New York and London: G. P. Putnam's Sons, 1892–1899), p. 477.

[3] Summary, *Manhattan Declaration* website, http://manhattandeclaration.org/#4.

of society, Pope Benedict said in the 2013 Celebration of the World Day of Peace, and he warned that the family's role as the "basic cell" of a healthy society cannot be ignored.

> The family has a natural vocation to promote life: it accompanies individuals as they mature and it encourages mutual growth and enrichment through caring and sharing.... The family is one of the indispensable social subjects for the achievement of a culture of peace. The rights of parents and their primary role in the education of their children in the area of morality and religion must be safeguarded. It is in the family that peacemakers, tomorrow's promoters of a culture of life and love, are born and nurtured.[4]

This converges with the State's interest in marriage as well. Those who want to redefine marriage deny that the State has an interest in marriage, and therefore any objection to changing marriage law comes from religiously informed people who are "intolerant". But the State's primary interest in marriage is to propagate future citizens of the State, for one thing. The small social units that are man-woman-child families create the next generation and subsequent generations that keep society going, and these units maintain social order.

The family also makes for a healthier economy by taking care of its children so the State doesn't need to provide for them and pass that expense on to taxpayers and responsibility to social service agencies of the State. It makes for a healthier, happier culture in many ways.

In April 2010, the *New York Times* ran a lengthy piece in its *Magazine* titled "Is Marriage Good for Your Health?" It opened with a focus on British epidemiologist William Farr's 1858 study of the "conjugal condition" of the people of France in three categories:

> the "married," consisting of husbands and wives; the "celibate," defined as the bachelors and spinsters who had never married; and finally the "widowed," those who had experienced the death of a spouse. Using birth, death and marriage records, Farr analyzed the relative mortality rates of the three groups at various ages. The work, a groundbreaking study that helped establish the field of medical statistics, showed that the

[4] Pope Benedict XVI, "Message of His Holiness Pope Benedict XVI for the Celebration of the World Day of Peace" (Jan. 1, 2013), no. 6, http://www.vatican.va/holy father/benedict_xvi/messages/peace/documents/hf_ben-xvi_mes_20121208_xlvi-world-day-peace_en.html.

> unmarried died from disease "in undue proportion" to their married counterparts. And the widowed, Farr found, fared worst of all.
>
> Farr's was among the first scholarly works to suggest that there is a health advantage to marriage and to identify marital loss as a significant risk factor for poor health. Married people, the data seemed to show, lived longer, healthier lives. "Marriage is a healthy estate," Farr concluded. "The single individual is more likely to be wrecked on his voyage than the lives joined together in matrimony."[5]

Then the *Times* proceeded to call Farr's study irrelevant "to the social realities of today's world" because it didn't include "couples living together, gay couples and the divorced, for instance".

So let's take a look at that, because Pope Paul VI predicted these social realities in his 1968 Encyclical *Humanae Vitae* in 1968—an encyclical known for the Pope's clarification of the Church's position on contraception. In fact, go back just a bit further, as Joseph Bottum did in *First Things* magazine on the 2008 anniversary of the encyclical.

> It's hard to remember all the joys we were told that contraception would bring, back in the day. For generations, from Victoria Woodhull all the way down to Margaret Sanger, birth-control activists had insisted that abortion would cease if we allowed access to contraception. In the 1965 decision *Griswold v. Connecticut*, the U.S. Supreme Court placed decisions about birth control at the center of the marriage bond. The smutty theaters, the back-room racks of pornography, the venereal diseases, the crushing down of young women into a life of timidity, the out-of-wedlock births, the masturbatory shame—all the sicknesses of a repressed culture would be swept away in the free love that contraception allows.
>
> *Free love*—forty years on, the phrase has a marvelously musty sound to it, like the fragile violets of a Victorian spinster's girlhood, pressed in the fading pages of her remembrance book. Things didn't work out quite the way we were promised. In fact, the results were pretty much what the pope had said they would be.[6]

Pope Paul predicted that with universal acceptance and use of contraception, men would lose respect for women and see them as objects for pleasure.

[5] Tara Parker-Pope, "Is Marriage Good for Your Health?" *New York Times Magazine*, Apr. 14, 2010, http://www.nytimes.com/2010/04/18/magazine/18marriage-t.html.

[6] Joseph Bottum, "The Anniversary of *Humanae Vitae*", *First Things*, July 25, 2008, http://www.firstthings.com/onthesquare/2008/07/the-anniversary-of-humanae-vit.

> Paul VI predicted, as well, that the institution of marriage would have trouble surviving "the conjugal infidelity" that contraception makes easy. Far from strengthening marriage as the Supreme Court seems to have imagined, the advent of birth control left marriage in tatters, as the sexual revolution roared through town. If many more people use contraception today than they used to—and do so certainly with less shame—then why have divorce, abortion, out-of-wedlock pregnancies, and venereal disease done nothing but increase since 1968?[7]

Another objectification he predicted was that people would come to "picture their bodies as somehow possessions, rather than as their actual being".[8]

There's no denying those are the "social realities" we're now dealing with, along with their consequences of dysfunction, depression, drug and alcohol use, and teen pregnancies among the generations to come after the Sixties.

In that hypersexualized society, the homosexual movement grew and sought first respect, then civil rights, and both happened over time. Scholar Ryan T. Anderson makes this point in a Heritage Foundation blog post challenging the demands for "marriage equality" on their face value. "In all 50 states, two people of the same sex can choose to live together, choose to join a religious community that blesses their relationship, and choose a workplace offering them various joint benefits. Many liberal houses of worship and progressive businesses have voluntarily decided to do so. There's nothing illegal about this. There's no ban on it."[9] Before the 2012 elections, some state legislators passed civil union laws on their own, without involving voters. New York was one.

> When New York became the sixth and by far the largest state to legalize same-sex marriage, ... it immediately transformed the national debate over the issue, legal experts said. With a population over 19 million—more than the combined population of the five states that currently allow gay marriage, plus the District of Columbia, where it is also legal—New York is poised to provide the most complete picture yet of the legal, social and economic consequences of gay marriage.[10]

[7] Ibid.

[8] Ibid.

[9] Ryan T. Anderson, "Obama, Equality, and Marriage", *The Foundry*, Jan. 24, 2013, http://blog.heritage.org/2013/01/24/obama-equality-and-same sex-marriage.

[10] "National Impact from New York Marriage Law: Experts", *Reuters*, June 24, 2011, http://www.reuters.com/article/2011/06/25/us-gaymarriage-new-york-impact-idUSTRE75O0DB20110625?feedType=RSS&feedName=domesticNews.

So this seemed to say this is a huge social experiment: "If a significant portion of those couples choose to marry, it could provide a wealth of new information about the practical economic effects of such legislation, from employment and retirement benefits to divorce rates and wedding and tourism industries...." A New York University Law School professor said: "It becomes less of an experiment the more information we have."[11]

## Social Consequences of Same-Sex Marriage

We have information. But even before it began emerging, a doctoral student published a rare argument on the Massachusetts Institute of Technology's online journal, *The Tech*, that considered the extended consequences of legally redefining marriage.

> The debate over whether the state ought to recognize gay marriages has thus far focused on the issue as one of civil rights. Such a treatment is erroneous because state recognition of marriage is not a universal right. States regulate marriage in many ways besides denying men the right to marry men, and women the right to marry women. Roughly half of all states prohibit first cousins from marrying, and all prohibit marriage of closer blood relatives, even if the individuals being married are sterile. In all states, it is illegal to attempt to marry more than one person, or even to pass off more than one person as one's spouse. Some states restrict the marriage of people suffering from syphilis or other venereal diseases. Homosexuals, therefore, are not the only people to be denied the right to marry the person of their choosing.[12]

The author is not equating homosexuals marrying with all the other scenarios mentioned in that paragraph. His is only saying that marriage has traditionally been heavily regulated for particular reasons of interest to the State.

> If the state must recognize a marriage of two men simply because they love one another, upon what basis can it deny marital recognition to a group of two men and three women, for example, or a sterile brother and sister who claim to love each other? Homosexual activists protest

[11] Ibid.

[12] Adam Kolasinski, "The Secular Case against Gay Marriage", *The Tech: Online Edition*, 124, no. 5 (Feb. 17, 2004), http://tech.mit.edu/V124/N5/kolasinski.5c.html.

> that they only want all couples treated equally. But why is sexual love between two people more worthy of state sanction than love between three, or five? When the purpose of marriage is procreation, the answer is obvious. If sexual love becomes the primary purpose, the restriction of marriage to couples loses its logical basis, leading to marital chaos.[13]

After the elections of 2012, when voters for the first time approved same-sex marriage legislation at the polls in three states, Ryan T. Anderson again challenged the "marriage equality" argument, elaborating on some of those points the MIT student made that were earlier more like thought experiments. If marriage is redefined, its goal posts will most certainly be moved, and its definition malleable. Anderson particularly addressed the argument that "marriage is simply whatever sort of relationship consenting adults—be they two or ten in number—want it to be; sexual or platonic, sexually exclusive or open, temporary or permanent".[14] Elsewhere he questions, "If so, how can redefining marriage for public purposes to include same-sex relationships be a demand of justice? A matter of basic fairness and equality? From the wide variety of interpersonal consensual relationships that adults can form, why should the state pick out same-sex ones?"[15]

In this ideological view, marital norms, even newly "evolved" ones, make no sense.

> There is no reason of principle why emotional union should be permanent. Or limited to two persons, rather than larger ensembles. Or sexual, much less sexually exclusive. Or inherently oriented to family life and shaped by its demands.
>
> If marriage isn't founded on a comprehensive union made possible by the sexual complementarity of a man and a woman, then why can't it occur among more than two people? If marital union isn't founded on such sexual acts, then why ought it be sexually exclusive? If marriage isn't a comprehensive union and has no intrinsic connection to children, then why ought it be permanent?[16]

[13] Ibid.

[14] Ryan T. Anderson, "Redefining Marriage Has Consequences", *The Heritage Foundation*, Mar. 26, 2013, http://www.heritage.org/research/commentary/2013/3/redefining-marriage-has-consequences.

[15] Ryan T. Anderson, "The Future of Marriage", *The Heritage Foundation*, Dec. 14, 2012, http://www.heritage.org/research/commentary/2012/12/the-future-of-marriage.

[16] Ibid.

These are important questions we need to engage in public debate—especially as the social consequences of these "genderless marriages" unfold, each with human persons and human dignity and identity at center.

For instance, there is the case of M.C., a little girl born in California in 2009 to a woman named Melissa. This story sounds like fiction but is sadly true. It's sad in and of itself. But when it led to a California State Senator pushing for a "Three-Parent Law" in that state, it got worse, potentially for every such case that would follow. Dr. Jennifer Roback Morse, founder of the Ruth Institute, wrote extensively on this case.

> Let us state an obvious fact: a same-sex couple cannot have a child unless someone gives them one, or part of one, namely, either an egg or a sperm. If two women, for instance, decide they want to have a baby, they must still involve a man in the process. They can use some form of artificial reproductive technology with sperm from a man who is unknown to them. Or, they can find an accommodating friend to have sex with one of them, or to donate his sperm.
>
> The question is this: how is the same-sex couple going to manage the relationship with this third party?[17]

In some cases, it winds up like this one, with "triple-parenting".

Here's how the California State Senator pushing for the "Three-Parent" bill summarized it in the briefest way possible, which made it all the more startling:

> [Sen.] Leno said inspiration for the bill came from a 2011 state appellate court case in which a young girl had two mothers. When one of the mothers was sent to prison and the other was hospitalized, the girl's biological father wished to care for her.
>
> The court, however, ruled the biological father could not be a legal guardian because of California's current law allowing only two parents per child.
>
> The state took custody of the child.[18]

Dr. Roback Morse adds the fuller explanation that peels back the illusions of a "new normal" that works if only everyone evolves into this artificial concept of parenthood that remains a social experiment under government control.

[17] Jennifer Roback Morse, "Why California's Three-Parent Law Was Inevitable", *The Witherspoon Institute: Public Discourse*, Sept. 10, 2012, http://www.thepublicdiscourse.com/2012/09/6197.

[18] NBC News, cited in ibid.

> Little M.C. had three parents, recognized under different parts of the law. Melissa counted as a mother because she gave birth to the child. Irene was married to Melissa when Melissa gave birth to M.C., so Irene counted as a presumed mother under a gender-neutral reading of the statute that was formerly used to establish paternity. José, the boyfriend who stabbed Irene, was not M.C.'s father. A man named Jesus was the biological father. Melissa had a relationship with him during one of her separations from Irene.
>
> No court ever denied that Jesus was a father. Nor did any court find him an unfit father in any way. So with Melissa in prison and Irene in the hospital, why couldn't the court simply give M.C. to Jesus, her biological father?
>
> The reason M.C. was placed in foster care was that the courts found that this would jeopardize the child's interest in reunification with Irene. Bear in mind that Irene was not the biological mother. She was not an adoptive mother. She had lived with Melissa and M.C. for about three or four weeks after the child was born.[19]

"The solution to this tragic case," Roback Morse continues, "is not to amend the law to allow three parents", but "to amend the law to remove the possibility of a person unrelated to the child, either by biology or adoption, being counted as a parent. The solution is to stop requiring a gender-neutral reading of a statute that is based on the biological, gendered facts of human reproduction."[20]

In December 2012, the Institute for American Values and the National Marriage Project released a report entitled "The President's Marriage Agenda for the Forgotten Sixty Percent", advancing what its title clearly says. The Institute for American Values stated its hope that the report would launch a new conversation on marriage, encouraging a political and cultural shift to engage and embrace a new vision of marriage and "child wellbeing" that would guide us to new frontiers. This vision, they hoped, would reverse the trend of declining marriage rates with its social costs, and it would encourage young people to "bond with one another and give their children the gift of their father and mother in a lasting marriage".[21]

The first and most glaring problem with this report was the absence of any questions or answers about the nature of the topic in the first

[19] Roback Morse, "California's Three-Parent Law".

[20] Ibid.

[21] Elizabeth Marquardt et al., "The President's Marriage Agenda for the Forgotten Sixty Percent", Institute for American Values and the National Marriage Project (Dec. 2012), http://www.stateofourunions.org/2012/presidents-marriage-agenda.php.

place. G.K. Chesterton said that when something is broken or in need of repair, before you go about tooling around with fixes to patch it up, you have to understand how it was meant to work in the first place.[22]

The central question completely overlooked in this political and cultural movement to change and redefine marriage was "What is Marriage?" Ryan T. Anderson, together with Sherif Girgis and Robert P. George, devoted in-depth discussion to that question and turned it into a thorough and definitive book on the issue, titled *What Is Marriage? Man and Woman: A Defense*.[23] The authors have broken out their succinct and reasoned argument into articles aimed at specific news events. Anderson's article in *Public Discourse* responded to "The President's Marriage Agenda" report with challenges.

> The report's fourth recommendation, "End Anonymous Fatherhood," notes that "the anonymous man who provided his sperm walks away with no obligation." Although a relatively small percentage of parents "use sperm donation or similar technologies to get pregnant, the cultural power of the idea that it's acceptable deliberately to create a fatherless child and for biological fathers to walk away from their children is real."
>
> The authors propose that the United States ban anonymity in sperm donation "and reinforce the consistent message that fathers matter." But how does marriage policy reinforce that message if it redefines marriage to say that mothers and fathers—one of each—are optional for marriage? How does redefining marriage to include lesbian relationships not further incentivize the type of anonymous sperm donation and resulting fatherless children that the authors protest?[24]

And while we're considering that, here's a news story that gives life and personal human drama to the social and thought experiments.

[22] "There has arisen in our time a most singular fancy: the fancy that when things go very wrong we need a practical man. It would be far truer to say, that when things go very wrong we need an unpractical man. Certainly, at least, we need a theorist. A practical man means a man accustomed to mere daily practice, to the way things commonly work. When things will not work, you must have the thinker, the man who has some doctrine about why they work at all." G.K. Chesterton, *What's Wrong with the World* (San Francisco: Ignatius Press, 1994), p. 19.

[23] Sherif Girgis, Ryan T. Anderson, and Robert P. George, *What Is Marriage? Man and Woman: A Defense* (New York: Encounter Books, 2012).

[24] Ryan T. Anderson, "Can the President Have a Marriage Agenda without Talking about What Marriage Is?" *The Witherspoon Institute: Public Discourse*, Dec. 18, 2012, http://www.thepublicdiscourse.com/2012/12/7437.

At the end of December 2012, news broke that a Craigslist sperm donor was being ordered to pay child support to a lesbian couple despite giving up all rights and obligations in writing before the child was born. The couple separated a year later but continued to "co-parent" the girl and seven siblings they had adopted over the years. The woman who bore the child lost her job, and her former partner was unable to provide support because of ill health, so the only parent registered in the state, the mother, applied for welfare. The Kansas Department of Children and Families insisted on the identity of the child's paternal father and then pressured him to provide financial support.[25]

In 2012, a group of religious leaders joined forces to support, promote, and protect marriage as the union of one man and one woman for the common good of society, the well-being of the couple, and certainly the children. They issued a letter voicing their concerns in support of marriage and religious liberty, which are bound together, they explained. What they wrote relates to all these issues, including the particular cases of M.C. and the sperm-donor father. They see or foresee conflicts where same-sex conduct is given the moral equivalence of natural marital conduct, affecting a cascading spectrum of society.

> These conflicts bear serious consequences. They will arise in a broad range of legal contexts, because altering the civil definition of "marriage" does not change one law, but hundreds, even thousands, at once. By a single stroke, every law where rights depend on marital status—such as employment discrimination, employment benefits, adoption, education, healthcare, elder care, housing, property, and taxation—will change so that same-sex sexual relationships must be treated as if they were marriage. That requirement, in turn, will apply to religious people and groups in the ordinary course of their many private or public occupations and ministries—including running schools, hospitals, nursing homes and other housing facilities, providing adoption and counseling services, and many others.[26]

[25] "Craigslist Sperm Donor Forced to Pay Child Support to Lesbian Couple—Despite Giving Up Parental Rights to the Baby BEFORE She Was Born", *Daily Mail Online*, Dec. 31, 2012, http://www.dailymail.co.uk/news/article-2255241/Sperm-donor-ordered-pay-child-support-lesbian-couple-despite-giving-rights-child.html.

[26] "Marriage and Religious Freedom: Fundamental Goods That Stand or Fall Together", Open Letter from Religious Leaders in the United States to All Americans (Jan. 12, 2012); accessed from http://www.usccb.org/issues-and-action/marriage-and-family/marriage/promotion-and-defense-of-marriage/upload/Marriage-and-Religious-Freedom.pdf.

That happened when Illinois legislators passed a civil unions bill during a lame-duck session, in spite of the state's bishops urging them to resist the measure. After it went into effect, the state's Department of Children and Family Services told Catholic Charities their foster care and adoption contracts would not be renewed. Catholic Charities was taken out of an essential social service because they would not bow to the State's demand to place children with homosexual couples.

Bishop Thomas Paprocki of Springfield, seat of the state government, said this: "The silver lining of this decision is that our Catholic Charities going forward will be able to focus on being more Catholic and more charitable, while less dependent on government funding and less encumbered by intrusive state policies."[27]

But soon after, the State intruded again, when lawmakers introduced legislation to turn that civil unions law into one that redefined marriage. Paprocki, a lawyer and adjunct professor at the Loyola University School of Law, testified before the Illinois Senate Executive Committee in early 2013, asking them to vote no on the bill called "The Religious Freedom and Marriage Fairness Act".[28] In that testimony, Paprocki said the bill failed to recognize certain truths about marriage. He also warned:

> It would enshrine in our law—and thus in public opinion and practice—three harmful ideas:
>
> 1. What essentially makes a marriage is romantic-emotional union.
> 2. Children do not need both a mother and a father.
> 3. The main purpose of marriage is adult satisfactions.[29]

Like Bishop Paprocki, Chicago's Cardinal Francis George issued a letter to be read at all the parishes in his archdiocese the first weekend of January 2013. The letter, cosigned by all the Chicago auxiliary bishops, similarly points out the repercussions of such a law:

[27] Manya A. Brachear, "3 Dioceses Drop Foster Care Lawsuit", *Chicago Tribune*, Nov. 15, 2011, http://articles.chicagotribune.com/2011-11-15/news/ct-met-catholic-charities-foster-care-20111115_1_civil-unions-act-catholic-charities-religious-freedom-protection.

[28] Paprocki's pastoral letter to his diocese said: "A more fraudulent title for this dangerous measure could not be imagined. The proposed law is, in truth, a grave assault upon both religious liberty and marriage." Bishop Thomas John Paprocki, "Bishop Paprocki Issues Letter on Same-Sex Marriage", Diocese of Springfield: Diocesan Blog, Text of Letter, Jan. 3, 2013, http://www.dio.org/blog/item/326-bishop-paprockis-letter-on-same-sex-marriage.html#sthash.V1KsW7OZ.dpbs.

[29] Ibid.

> This proposed legislation will have long term consequences because laws teach; they tell us what is socially acceptable and what is not, and most people conform to the dictates of their respective society.... What happens next? If we ignore in law the natural complementarity of man and woman in creation, then the natural family is undermined.... When the ways of nature and nature's God conflict with civil law, society is in danger.[30]

## The Nature of Marriage Preexists Church or State

Cardinal George, who is a preeminent philosopher and scholar prelate in the Church in America, continued his argument against the proposed Illinois "gay marriage" law in the *Catholic New World* archdiocesan newspaper, which hit the secular news pretty fast when he said, "The Legislature might just as well repeal the law of gravity." But here's the context, in his column "Legislation Creating 'Same-Sex' Marriage: What's at Stake?"

> Basically, the nature of marriage is not a religious question. Marriage comes to us from nature. Christ sanctifies marriage as a sacrament for the baptized, giving it significance beyond its natural reality; the State protects marriage because it is essential to family and to the common good of society. But neither Church nor State invented marriage, and neither can change its nature....
>
> [N]o matter how strong a friendship or deep a love between persons of the same sex might be, it is physically impossible for two men, or two women, to consummate a marital union. Even in civil law, non-consummation of a marriage is reason for annulment.
>
> Sexual relations between a man and a woman are naturally and necessarily different from sexual relations between same-sex partners. This truth is part of the common sense of the human race. It was true before the existence of either Church or State, and it will continue to be true when there is no State of Illinois and no United States of America. A proposal to change this truth about marriage in civil law is less a threat to religion than it is an affront to human reason and the common good of society. It means we are all to pretend to accept something we know

[30] Francis Cardinal George, O.M.I., et al., "'Same-Sex Marriage': What Do Nature and Nature's God Say?" (Jan. 1, 2013), http://www.ilcatholic.org/wp-content/uploads/SSMLetter-BulletinsJan2013.pdf.

> is physically impossible. The Legislature might just as well repeal the law of gravity.[31]

Cardinal George raises the important question virtually ignored in the public debate, "Why this law?" Why now? His answers are essential to understand what society and its institutions and individuals are going through in this battle.

> Since all the strictly legal consequences of natural marriage are already given to same-sex partners in civil unions, what is now at stake in this question for some homosexually oriented people is self-respect and full societal acceptance of their sexual activities. Because fair-minded people cannot approve of hatred or disdain of others, "same-sex marriage" becomes for many a well-intentioned and good-hearted response to help others be happy. But marriage is a public commitment with a responsibility that involves more than the personal happiness of two adults. Inventing "civil rights" that contradict natural rights does not solve a problem of personal unhappiness.[32]

The "rights" language has helped the movement to redefine marriage, along with a campaign claiming it as a human right or civil right, and Cardinal George correctly acknowledges that Americans are fair-minded and tolerant and don't want to deny anyone their rights. But just as the "semantic gymnastics" worked for the abortion movement, the language engineering that separates words from their meaning is working for this movement and will continue to do so unless challenged and clarified.

In the name of tolerance, people of faith are not being tolerated. And their rights are being denied.

Ken Blackwell, Visiting Professor at Liberty University School of Law, and former U.S. Ambassador to the U.N. Human Rights Commission, said the marriage battle is creating coalitions across lines of race, creed, and color. Blackwell elaborated on that claim, eloquently, in an open letter to General Colin Powell after Powell appeared on a news program and implied that, as Blackwell put it, "those of us, in the GOP who defend life, protect traditional marriage and advance

[31] Francis Cardinal George, O.M.I., "Legislation Creating 'Same-Sex' Marriage: What's at Stake?" *Catholic New World*, Jan. 6–9, 2013, http://catholicnewworld.com/cnwonline/2013/0106/cardinal.aspx.

[32] Ibid.

religious liberty are intolerant". The title of the letter was "Who Are the Intolerant?"[33]

Blackwell pointed out how obvious it was to anyone watching the Democratic National Convention in August 2012 that when a floor vote was called for inserting God back into the party platform, a majority of the voice votes clearly shouted "No". The voice vote was called for two more times, with the same result. It was fudged by the convention chairman and taken as a "Yes" to the objection of loudly dissenting delegates. Blackwell says: "Three times they denied God. Denied Him Thrice!"

> What does it mean for a party to reject God? First of all, it means they must reject life itself. We know that God is the author of life. Speaker after speaker demanded abortion, and more of it. No longer would Democrats have any hesitation about abortion. No longer would they say, as Bill Clinton said, it should be safe, legal, and rare.
>
> The Democratic Platform dropped those last two words, and rare.... [An] NPR reporter ... pointed out that 30% of Democrats are pro-life. And who would those pro-life Democrats be? Disproportionately, they are black and Hispanic voters. And Catholic and Evangelical voters.[34]

Blackwell made challenging points about abortion, religious freedom, and marriage as issues important to these groups of citizens committed to the defense of social moral values they share.

> In 1866, historian Allen Guelzo reports, Tennessee recorded thousands more marriages than in the previous four years. That's because newly freed black couples were walking to Tennessee to have their marriages recognized by law.
>
> How tragic, then, that the Charlotte convention came out against marriage, too. They say they only want to add to the number of happily married couples by allowing men to marry men and women to marry women. But we know that wherever these counterfeit marriages have been recognized, true marriage declines. All over Northern Europe, when civil unions were enforced, true marriage ceased to be that special, God-ordained union it has always been.

[33] Ken Blackwell, "Who Are the Intolerant? Ken Blackwell Writes an Open Letter to General Powell", Jan. 15, 2013, article provided by Townhall, http://townhall.com/columnists/kenblackwell/2013/01/14/an-open-letter-to-general-powell-n1488741/page/full.

[34] Ibid.

Blackwell continued his impassioned case.

> In North Carolina—just three months before the Democratic Convention met in Charlotte—black voters provid[ed] the winning margin for a state referendum that affirmed true marriage. There was no stronger group of voters supporting marriage than black voters.
>
> ... Consider how much has changed and how fast. In 1996, the Defense of Marriage Act passed Congress by an overwhelming vote. It won 342 votes in the House and 85 votes in the Senate. It was so strong[ly] supported that this law would have been approved if there were no Republicans in either House of Congress. That's why President Bill Clinton felt he had no choice but to sign it.
>
> President Obama has refused to enforce the Defense of Marriage Act and pledges to repeal it.... If two men can marry, why not three? If gays and lesbians can marry, what about bi-sexual persons and persons who have sought to change their sex? Why can't they have one spouse of either sex?
>
> After slavery, after Jim Crow, after the KKK, it is fair to say that among the worst things visited upon black Americans have been the targeting of our families by abortionists and the effort to end marriage.
>
> That is why we are in a crisis. This is what happens when a major party rejects God.[35]

The social moral issues come first before a good and just nation can talk about or make policy decisions on taxes, the economy, global trade, and so on.

That's the message drafters of the *Manhattan Declaration* wanted the document and ensuing movement to embody. It's not politically partisan; it's morally grounded in Christian values, and primary among them are the sanctity of life, the preservation of traditional marriage, and the protection of conscience rights of religiously informed citizens.

This is from the section on Marriage:

> In Scripture, the creation of man and woman, and their one-flesh union as husband and wife, is the crowning achievement of God's creation. In the transmission of life and the nurturing of children, men and women joined as spouses are given the great honor of being partners with God Himself. Marriage then, is the first institution of human society—indeed it is the institution on which all other human institutions have their foundation....

[35] Ibid.

> To strengthen families, we must stop glamorizing promiscuity and infidelity and restore among our people a sense of the profound beauty, mystery, and holiness of faithful marital love.... We must work in the legal, cultural, and religious domains to instill in young people a sound understanding of what marriage is, what it requires, and why it is worth the commitment and sacrifices that faithful spouses make.
>
> The impulse to redefine marriage in order to recognize same-sex and multiple partner relationships is a symptom, rather than the cause, of the erosion of the marriage culture. It reflects a loss of understanding of the meaning of marriage as embodied in our civil and religious law and in the philosophical tradition that contributed to shaping the law. Yet it is critical that the impulse be resisted, for yielding to it would mean abandoning the possibility of restoring a sound understanding of marriage and, with it, the hope of rebuilding a healthy marriage culture. It would lock into place the false and destructive belief that marriage is all about romance and other adult satisfactions, and not, in any intrinsic way, about procreation and the unique character and value of acts and relationships whose meaning is shaped by their aptness for the generation, promotion and protection of life.[36]

The section of the *Manhattan Declaration* devoted to "Life" is packed with wisdom and is concise and relatively short. The section on "Marriage" is full of insight, ready to identify and tackle modern cultural battles, and at least twice as long.

> We call on the entire Christian community to resist sexual immorality, and at the same time refrain from disdainful condemnation of those who yield to it....

Both parts of that statement are important.

> We further acknowledge that there are sincere people who disagree with us, and with the teaching of the Bible and Christian tradition, on questions of sexual morality and the nature of marriage.... They fail to understand, however, that marriage is made possible by the sexual complementarity of man and woman, and that the comprehensive, multi-level sharing of life that marriage is includes bodily unity of the sort that unites husband and wife biologically as a reproductive unit. This is because the body is no mere extrinsic instrument of the human person, but truly part of the personal reality of the human being. Human beings are not merely

[36] "Marriage", *Manhattan Declaration*, pp. 4–5, http://manhattandeclaration.org/man_dec_resources/Manhattan_Declaration_full_text.pdf.

> centers of consciousness or emotion, or minds, or spirits, inhabiting non-personal bodies. The human person is a dynamic unity of body, mind, and spirit....
>
> We understand that many of our fellow citizens, including some Christians, believe that the historic definition of marriage as the union of one man and one woman is a denial of equality or civil rights. They wonder what to say in reply to the argument that asserts that no harm would be done to them or to anyone if the law of the community were to confer upon two men or two women who are living together in a sexual partnership the status of being "married." It would not, after all, affect their own marriages, would it?[37]

The drafters succinctly make the case that it would affect marriage as an institution and open it to an expansion of marriage law practically unimaginable, but logical and undeniable.

> The truth is that marriage is not something abstract or neutral that the law may legitimately define and re-define to please those who are powerful and influential.
>
> No one has a civil right to have a non-marital relationship treated as a marriage. Marriage is an objective reality—a covenantal union of husband and wife—that it is the duty of the law to recognize and support for the sake of justice and the common good. If it fails to do so, genuine social harms follow.
>
> And so it is out of *love* (not "animus") and prudent *concern for the common good* (not "prejudice"), that we pledge to labor ceaselessly to preserve the legal definition of marriage as the union of one man and one woman and to rebuild the marriage culture. How could we, as Christians, do otherwise? The Bible teaches us that marriage is a central part of God's creation covenant. Indeed, the union of husband and wife mirrors the bond between Christ and his church. And so just as Christ was willing, out of love, to give Himself up for the church in a complete sacrifice, we are willing, lovingly, to make whatever sacrifices are required of us for the sake of the inestimable treasure that is marriage.[38]

## Pope Benedict's Concerns for Marriage and Family

Over and over, time and again, Pope Benedict XVI addressed the deterioration of a culture that once valued marriage and thrived on intact

[37] Ibid., pp. 5–6.

[38] Ibid., pp. 6–7 (emphasis in original).

families. To those who say that was a bygone era, and the current climate of free sexual license and unfettered sexual expression, claimed even by governing bodies as matters of justice and human rights, is the inevitable trajectory of modern people and their certain future, Pope Benedict said he heard them, understood why they say that, but he suggested another way. He recalled them to what they had forgotten and challenged them to think ideas through to their logical conclusion—and to how they are related.

Here's just one example: At the end of 2012, in his annual year-end address to the Roman Curia, Pope Benedict engaged contemporary European Catholic thinkers on the biblical basis for gender, identity, and parenthood as it affects proposed marriage laws in France. Pope Benedict commented:

> While up to now we regarded a false understanding of the nature of human freedom as one cause of the crisis of the family, it is now becoming clear that the very notion of being—of what being human really means—is being called into question....
>
> These [questions and] words lay the foundation for what is put forward today under the term "gender" as a new philosophy of sexuality. According to this philosophy, sex is no longer a given element of nature, that man has to accept and personally make sense of: it is a social role that we choose for ourselves....
>
> People dispute the idea that they have a nature, given by their bodily identity, that serves as a defining element of the human being. They deny their nature and decide that it is not something previously given to them, but that they make it for themselves....
>
> Man calls his nature into question. From now on he is merely spirit and will. *The manipulation of nature, which we deplore today where our environment is concerned*, now becomes man's fundamental choice where *he himself* is concerned....
>
> But if there is no pre-ordained duality of man and woman in creation, then neither is the family any longer a reality established by creation. Likewise, the child has lost the place he had occupied hitherto and the dignity pertaining to him.... [T]he child has become an object to which people have a right and which they have a right to obtain. When the freedom to be creative becomes the freedom to create oneself, then necessarily the Maker Himself is denied and ultimately man too is stripped of his dignity as a creature of God, as the image of God at the core of his being. The defence of the family is about man himself. And it becomes

> clear that when God is denied, human dignity also disappears. Whoever defends God is defending man.[39]

At the beginning of 2013, while the French legislature and British Parliament were in the process of passing same-sex marriage laws, the Vatican's Pontifical Council for the Family held a press conference to highlight the best of the 2012 Milan family conference and promote the next one to be held in Philadelphia. It was fortuitous timing, because whole movements of people on different continents rallying to defend natural marriage law were handed decisions by lawmakers that seemed to hand them defeat after defeat.

Council president Archbishop Vincenzo Paglia said that the Seventh World Meeting of Families in Milan showed the vital force families represent in society, in spite of appearances to the contrary in the popular culture.

> The statistics are unanimous in pointing out that the family is the first place of safety, refuge, and support for life and remains at the top of the vast majority of young person's wishes. In Italy, for example, around 80% of young people say that they prefer marriage (whether it be civil or religious) and only 20% would choose co-habitation.... In France, surveys indicate that 77% want to build their family life, staying with the same person throughout their lives.... On the other hand, the need for family is inscribed on the human heart, since God tells us "It is not good for the man to be alone".[40]

But he was realistic about what's happening across the world.

> This profound truth, which marks human life so radically, seems to take a beating from counter culture.... There is an escalation in the race to individualism that is breaking up the family as well as other forms of society. That is why the breakdown of the family is the first problem of contemporary society.... It is true that much of contemporary Western History has been conceived as a liberation from every bond: from

[39] Pope Benedict XVI, "Address of His Holiness Benedict XVI on the Occasion of Christmas Greetings to the Roman Curia" (Dec. 21, 2012), http://www.vatican.va/holy_father/benedict_xvi/speeches/2012/december/documents/hf_ben-xvi_spe_20121221_auguri-curia_en.html (emphasis added).

[40] "Archbishop Paglia: The Family Continues to Be the Fundamental 'Resource' of Our Society", *News.va: The Vatican Today*, Feb. 4, 2013, http://www.news.va/en/news/the-family-is-good-news.

> ties to others and thus the family, from any responsibility toward the other. It is also true that bonds have, sometimes, oppressed individuality. But today, the vertigo of solitude with its cult of "me", free from any attachment ... and the disorientation caused by globalization further accentuate our becoming locked within ourselves and the temptation of self-absorption.[41]

Archbishop Paglia said the Church is concerned with the current crisis in marriage and the family, because she is aware that men and women today are "often alone, lacking love, parenting, and support".

> The Church, an "expert in humanity" knows well ... the high price of the fragility of the family, which is paid mainly by the children (born and unborn), by the elderly, and by the ill.... At times in various historical periods there have been transformations, even profound ones, in the institution of the family. But it has never abandoned its "genome", its deep dimension ... its being as an institution formed by a man, a woman, and children. That is why ... an even more vigorous defence of the family is urgent, so that it might be placed—and quickly—at the centre of politics, the economy, and culture, in the different countries as well as in the different international organizations, even involving believers of other religious traditions and all persons of good will.[42]

There were several buzzwords in that message to reveal the Church's sense of urgency on this issue that started slipping away fast through successful campaigns by the same-sex marriage movement to change minds and laws more rapidly in 2012 and into 2013. The vigorous defense of the family was already in place for years by different organizations, religious traditions, and "persons of good will". This was the case especially in the battles over California's Proposition 8 ballot initiative upholding the definition of marriage as between one man and one woman. The Catholic bishops were active and outspoken in defense of it, and the Church of Latter Day Saints took a leading role in campaigning for it. The Union of Orthodox Jewish Congregations of America, Eastern Orthodox Church, Evangelical groups, and notably Pastor Rick Warren supported Proposition 8. And the American Family Association, Focus on the Family, and the National Organization for Marriage also endorsed the measure.

[41] Ibid.

[42] Ibid.

When the vote was broken down demographically, 70 percent of African Americans voted to ban same-sex marriages in California.[43] Some Proposition 8 supporters viewed the black vote as proof that same-sex marriage is a moral rather than a civil rights issue.

## Persons and Acts

It's also an issue deeply rooted in the understanding of what it means to be a fully integrated human being, and not a conscious "self" inhabiting a body that's merely an instrument, the dualistic view Plato held. Princeton professor Robert P. George pointed to this underlying philosophy in an interview with the Christian news magazine *World*. When interviewer Marvin Olasky asked George why marriage today centers so much on "feeling" right, George responded:

> It's part of a larger trend towards identifying the good or the valuable with pleasing experiences and psychological satisfactions. This helps to explain not only the decline of sexual morality in our culture, but also the widespread use of recreational drugs. Many people (including more than a few Christians) have come to view themselves as consciousnesses (or, for people who retain some level of religious self-understanding, as "souls") that inhabit bodies. Since the body is regarded as merely instrumental, rather than as part of the personal reality of the human being (considered as a dynamic unity of body, mind, and spirit), moral constraints of any sort on "nonharmful" drugs or "nonharmful" sexual practices of "consenting adults" seem arbitrary and even irrational.[44]

That understanding of human nature and the nature of marriage which George describes answers pointed and increasingly challenging questions about why two people of the same gender who truly love each other can't enjoy the same recognition of their relationship as a man and a woman.

When San Francisco–based, U.S. District Court Judge Vaughn Walker ruled that California's voter-approved ban on same-sex marriage violates the U.S. Constitution and overturned Proposition 8, media

[43] Shelby Grad, "Seventy Percent of African Americans Backed Prop. 8, Exit Poll Finds", *Los Angeles Times*, L.A. Now, Nov. 5, 2008, http://latimesblogs.latimes.com/lanow/2008/11/70-of-african-a.html, citing the Associated Press.

[44] Marvin Olasky, "Body and Soul: Princeton Scholar Robert P. George on the Philosophy that Underlies Abortion, Drug Abuse, Euthanasia, and the Widespread Decline of Sexual Morality", interview, *World Magazine*, Mar. 5, 2005, http://www.worldmag.com/2005/03/body_and_soul.

coverage and therefore much of the public debate missed the fundamental argument for the defense of marriage. The voters voted, and they voted wrong, ruled this judge.

Walker's ruling stems from a lawsuit filed by two gay couples who claimed the law violated their civil rights. In a press conference, one of those plaintiffs said the ruling by Walker speaks to fundamental American values of freedom and fairness. He said a government by, of, and for the people cannot discriminate against the people.

But the government of the people, exercised by the people, and for the people in the electoral process when they voted on this issue was overturned by this unelected judge. So these arguments were rhetorical and fundamentally not accurate.

In his ruling, Walker repeatedly argued in his decision that banning same-sex marriage amounted to sex discrimination because some individuals are denied the right to marry others based solely on their gender. In his 136-page ruling, Walker wrote, "Excluding same-sex couples from marriage is simply not rationally related to a legitimate state interest."[45] This is not true.

Legal scholar William C. Duncan explains why in a document called "The State Interests in Marriage", published in the *Ave Maria Law Review*.

> The most common state interest discussed in same-sex marriage case law relates to procreation, either the interest in encouraging procreation for the sake of ensuring the continuation of society or the interest in responsible procreation. In one of the earliest opinions, arising from a challenge to Washington's marriage law, the court asserted, "The fact remains that marriage exists as a protected legal institution primarily because of societal values associated with the propagation of the human race." The court also said that the state's failure to redefine marriage to include same-sex couples "is based upon the state's recognition that our society as a whole views marriage as the appropriate and desirable forum for procreation and the rearing of children." The court rejected the contention that the fact that some married couples do not have children defeats this interest, noting that "[t]hese ... are exceptional situations."[46]

[45] Jesse McKinley and John Schwartz, "Court Rejects Same-Sex Marriage Ban in California", *New York Times*, U.S. Section, Aug. 4, 2010, http://www.nytimes.com/2010/08/05/us/05prop.html.

[46] William C. Duncan, "The State Interests in Marriage", *Ave Maria Law Review* 2, no. 1 (2004): 154, http://marriagelawfoundation.org/publications/Ave%20Maria%201.pdf, citing *Singer v. Hara*, 522 P. 2d 1187, 1195 (Wash. Ct. App. 1974).

This is only one of many available accounts of court cases citing state interest in marriage.

> Similarly, the Ninth Circuit noted that "homosexual marriages never produce offspring." In a dissent to the Supreme Court of Hawaii's decision that marriage is a form of sex discrimination, Judge Heen stated his belief that the purpose of the marriage law is "to promote and protect propagation."
>
> In the Vermont same-sex marriage case, the state argued that its marriage law protected the state's interest in "furthering the link between procreation and child rearing." By "promoting a permanent commitment between couples who have children to ensure that their offspring are considered legitimate and receive ongoing parental support" and counteracting a message that fathers and mothers "are mere surplusage to the functions of procreation and child rearing," the state can "send a public message that procreation and child rearing are intertwined."[47]

Such precedent and this understanding of marriage in nature and law were subsumed in the Girgis, Anderson, George book *What Is Marriage? Man and Woman: A Defense.* "Conjugal marriage laws reinforce the idea that the union of husband and wife is, on the whole, the most appropriate environment for rearing children—an ideal supported by the best available social science. Recognizing same-sex relationships as marriages would legally abolish that ideal."[48]

Defending natural, conjugal marriage this way does not at all discriminate against homosexual persons or those promoting same-sex marriage. The issue is what marriage is and may be and for what purpose, as recognized by law. "Both views make claims about which relationships to honor and encourage as marriages—and, by implication, which relationships not to recognize in this way", the authors write.

> The revisionist view, at least in the version currently most represented in public debates, would honor and privilege both monogamous heterosexual and same-sex unions but not polyamorous ones. And both views are disputed. There is no neutral marriage policy.
>
> But that is true not only of marriage. Settling other policies also requires controversial moral stances on issues where theologies clash:

[47] Ibid., pp. 155–56, citing *Adams v. Howerton*, 673 F.2d 1036, 1043 (9th Cir. 1982); *Baehr v. Lewin*, 852 P.2d 44, 73 n.8 (Haw. 1993; Heen, J., dissenting); and *Baker v. Vermont*, 744 A.2d 864, 881 (Vt. 1999).

[48] Girgis et al., *What Is Marriage?* p. 58.

> affirmative action, abortion, assisted suicide and euthanasia, poverty relief, capital punishment, torture, nuclear deterrence, and more. That does not mean that the state must keep silent on these matters. It does mean that citizens owe it to each other to explain the reasons for their views with clarity and candor.[49]

And charity is also needed, as Vatican II emphasized in *Inter Mirifica*, the decree on social communications. "Since public opinion exercises the greatest power and authority today in every sphere of life, both private and public, every member of society must fulfill the demands of justice and charity in this area."[50] "[T]here must be full respect for the laws of morality and for the legitimate rights and dignity of the individual. For not all knowledge is helpful, but 'it is charity that edifies.'"[51]

## Let's Be Clear:

1. **Gender is a dimension of our embodied humanity.** Gender and sex cannot be separated—they are two sides of the same coin. In other words, you can't be a man born in a woman's body, or vice versa. "Everyone, man and woman, should acknowledge and accept his sexual *identity*. Physical, moral, and spiritual *difference* and *complementarity* are oriented toward the goods of marriage and the flourishing of family life."[52]
2. **Everybody is called to live out their sexuality in a chaste context.** It is only in the context of marriage that sexual activity between two persons is appropriate. Sexual proclivity does not need to lead to sexual expression.[53]
3. **Marriage is a covenant between a man and a woman** who promise before God and society to enter into a union that is exclusive, mutual, lifelong, and open to new life. Those who propose that the purpose of marriage is only the emotional satisfaction of the couple are missing the point of marriage.

[49] Ibid., p. 96.

[50] Second Vatican Council, *Inter Mirifica*, Decree on the Media of Social Communications (Dec. 4, 1963), no. 8.

[51] Ibid., no. 5, citing 1 Cor 8:1.

[52] *Catechism of the Catholic Church*, no. 2333 (emphasis in original).

[53] Ibid., nos. 2337–50.

To choose someone of the same sex for one's sexual activity is to annul the rich symbolism and meaning, not to mention the goals, of the Creator's sexual design. Homosexual activity is not a complementary union, able to transmit life; and so it thwarts the call to a life of that form of self-giving which the Gospel says is the essence of Christian living.[54]

4. **Marriage is a reality rooted in the order of nature, and it is not the creation of the State or the Church.** Thus, neither the State nor the Church can change the definition of marriage, despite how many people might petition for its change.

The word "marriage" isn't simply a label that can be attached to different types of relationships. Instead, "marriage" reflects a deep reality—the reality of the unique, fruitful, lifelong union that is only possible between a man and a woman. Just as oxygen and hydrogen are essential to water, sexual difference is essential to marriage. The attempt to "redefine" marriage to include two persons of the same sex denies the reality of what marriage is. It is as impossible as trying to "redefine" water to include oxygen and nitrogen.[55]

5. **No two people of the same gender have the "right" to marry each other.** Homosexual marriage is not a civil rights issue, despite how much the homosexual movement claims it is.

The "right to marry" is the right to enter into a very particular kind of relationship having distinct characteristics that serve important social purposes; the "right to marry" is *not* the right to enter a relationship that is not a marriage, and then force others by law to treat that relationship as if it were a marriage. Advocates for same-sex "marriage" ignore this distinction. Far from serving the cause of civil rights, redefining marriage would threaten the civil right of religious freedom.[56]

[54] Congregation for the Doctrine of the Faith, *Letter to the Bishops of the Catholic Church on the Pastoral Care of Homosexual Persons* (Oct. 1, 1986), no. 7, http://www.vatican.va/roman_curia/congregations/cfaith/documents/rc_con_cfaith_doc_19861001_homosexual-persons_en.html.

[55] USCCB, *Frequently Asked Questions about the Defense of Marriage*, "The Meaning of Marriage and Sexual Difference", no. 4, http://www.usccb.org/issues-and-action/marriage-and-family/marriage/promotion-and-defense-of-marriage/frequently-asked-questions-on-defense-of-marriage.cfm#m4.

[56] Ibid., "The Common Good and Human Dignity", no. 11, http://www.usccb.org/issues-and-action/marriage-and-family/marriage/promotion-and-defense-of-marriage/frequently-asked-questions-on-defense-of-marriage.cfm#m11.

6. **Legalizing homosexual unions would negatively impact the institution of marriage as understood by the Church.**

> Marriage has great public significance.... And laws always promote a vision of "the good life." Because of this, redefining civil "marriage" to include two persons of the same sex would have far-reaching consequences in society. Law is a teacher, and such a law would teach many bad lessons ... such as the following: that marriage is only about the romantic fulfillment of adults ...; that mothers and fathers are wholly interchangeable and, in turn, that gender is inconsequential ...; that same-sex sexual conduct is not merely morally permissible, but a positive good equal in moral value to marital sex.[57]

7. **At the same time, in our personal dealings we should always remember to be respectful of people who experience homosexual attractions.** "*Every single human person* has great inviolable dignity and worth, including those who experience same-sex attraction. All persons should be treated with respect, sensitivity, and love. The Church calls *everyone* to a life of holiness and chastity, and to live in accord with God's will for their lives."[58]

[57] Ibid., "The Meaning of Marriage & Sexual Difference", no. 9, http://www.usccb.org/issues-and-action/marriage-and-family/marriage/promotion-and-defense-of-marriage/frequently-asked-questions-on-defense-of-marriage.cfm#m9.

[58] Ibid., "The Common Good and Human Dignity", no. 3, http://www.usccb.org/issues-and-action/marriage-and-family/marriage/promotion-and-defense-of-marriage/frequently-asked-questions-on-defense-of-marriage.cfm#m3.

# Chapter 5

# Dignity of Conscience: Religious Liberty

*A sense of the dignity of the human person has been impressing itself more and more deeply on the consciousness of contemporary man, and the demand is increasingly made that men should act on their own judgment, enjoying and making use of a responsible freedom, not driven by coercion but motivated by a sense of duty. The demand is likewise made that constitutional limits should be set to the powers of government, in order that there may be no encroachment on the rightful freedom of the person and of associations. This demand for freedom in human society chiefly regards the quest for the values proper to the human spirit. It regards, in the first place, the free exercise of religion in society.*[1]

—Vatican II, *Dignitatis Humanae*

*We all declare for liberty; but in using the same word we do not all mean the same thing. With some the word liberty may mean for each man to do as he pleases with himself, and the product of his labor; while with others, the same word may mean for some men to do as they please with other men, and the product of other men's labor. Here are two, not only different, but incompatible things, called by the same name—liberty.*[2]

—Abraham Lincoln

In August 2011, the Department of Health and Human Services (HHS) made public its intention to issue a mandate requiring insurance policies to provide for contraceptive services, including sterilization and

[1] Second Vatican Council, *Dignitatis Humanae* (Dec. 7, 1965), no. 1.

[2] Abraham Lincoln, "Address at Sanitary Fair, Baltimore, Maryland" (Apr. 18, 1864), in Abraham Lincoln Association, *The Collected Works of Abraham Lincoln*, ed. Roy P. Basler, vol. 7 (New Brunswick, N.J.: Rutgers University Press, 1953), pp. 301–2. Reprinted by permission of the Abraham Lincoln Association.

abortion-inducing drugs intended to prevent or terminate human life. Then the department announced it would receive and consider comments on that plan. Attorneys for the Dominican Sisters of the Congregation of Saint Cecilia sent HHS a letter:

> In their 151-year history, the Nashville Dominicans have, with the help of God, survived a Civil War on their doorstep, deadly epidemics, devastating floods, economic depression and tumultuous social upheaval. *Today, however, they face a new, more insidious threat—their own government.* Should HHS persist in implementing ... its contraceptive mandate without major modifications, the Congregation will be forced to curtail its mission. What war and disease could not do to the Congregation, the government of the United States will do. It will shut them down.[3]

This unprecedented threat from government would have unimaginable consequences for the nation's institutions—church-sponsored health care centers, universities, schools, charitable organizations, social ministries—and individuals, with tremendous impact on society and the common good. When they were devising this plan to begin with, HHS did not consult the nation's largest provider of health care services, Catholic hospitals and medical centers and institutions. During that "window of time" for public comment on the HHS mandate proposal, the administration of President Barack Obama, and the president himself, heard plenty from religious leaders, heads of organizations, professionals, and individuals.

The National Catholic Bioethics Center issued a letter calling out HHS for "treating pregnancy as a disease that should be prevented", which "is medically, socially, and anthropologically inaccurate and sexually biased. By treating pregnancy as a disease to be prevented one can only conclude that the treatment for such a 'disease' is an abortion."[4] The NCBC called the proposed rule unconstitutional.

In the waning hours of "public comment", the University of Notre Dame joined the swelling chorus of voices when President Fr. John

[3] "ACLJ: HHS Rule Violates Religious Freedom and Conscience Rights", *American Center for Law and Justice*, Sept. 30, 2011, http://aclj.org/pro-life/aclj-hhs-rule-violates-religious-freedom-conscience-rights (emphasis added).

[4] "The NCBC Expresses Extreme Dismay that Fact-Based Testimony on the Perils of President Obama's Contraceptive Mandate Have Been Ignored", National Catholic Bioethics Center: Resources, Jan. 27, 2012, http://www.ncbcenter.org/page.aspx?pid=1263, citing "NCBC Provides Testimony to Health and Human Services on Coverage of 'Preventive Services'", http://www.ncbcenter.org/page.aspx?pid=482&ncs1277=0.

Jenkins wrote a letter to HHS Secretary Kathleen Sebelius that the mandate places the school in the "impossible position" of having to defy Church teaching. The mandate "would compel Notre Dame to either pay for contraception and sterilization in violation of the Church's moral teaching, or to discontinue our employee and student health-care plans in violation of the Church's social teaching", Fr. Jenkins said.[5]

John Garvey, president of The Catholic University of America, also weighed in, saying that complying with the mandate for employers to provide access to abortion-inducing contraceptive drugs would mean "helping our students do things that we teach them, in our classes and in our sacraments, are sinful—sometimes gravely so. It seems to us that a proper respect for religious liberty would warrant an exemption for our university and other institutions."[6]

Garvey added: "It does not take a college education to see the hypocrisy in offering to pay for the very services we condemn in our theology classes and seek forgiveness for in our sacraments. It should not be the business of the federal government to force Catholic schools and other Catholic institutions into such a collective violation of our own conscientious beliefs."[7]

An odd alignment of events occurred a few months later that brought this "issuance" and two separate but related ones to an apex.

## The Defiance of Faith

In 2011, the Supreme Court of the United States heard a pivotal case known as *Hosanna-Tabor* that concerned the Church-State separation. An opinion piece in the *Washington Post* used strong language to describe the government's overreach in the case.

> From homeland security to healthcare, the federal government now has the power to reach further than ever into American society. But so far, the feds have sensibly stayed out of the business of appointing religious leaders.

[5] Rev. John I. Jenkins, C.S.C., Letter to the Honorable Kathleen Sebelius, Sept. 28, 2011, University of Notre Dame, http://president.nd.edu/assets/50056/comments_from_rev_john_i_jenkins_notre_dame_3_.pdf.

[6] John Garvey, "HHS's Birth-Control Rules Intrude on Catholic Values", *Washington Post*, Sept. 30, 2011, http://articles.washingtonpost.com/2011-09-30/opinions/35273200_1_catholic-charities-catholic-hospitals-health-plans.

[7] Ibid.

> Now, in a stunning about-face, the Obama Administration has urged the Supreme Court to allow courts to decide virtually any dispute between a church and its ministers. In the administration's view, juries and judges, not congregations and bishops, should have the final say on who is fit for religious ministry. Fundamental questions of theology would be resolved in the same way as slip-and-fall cases. Plaintiffs' lawyers would go into a religious feeding frenzy.
>
> The DOJ [Department of Justice] made this astounding declaration in its brief for a Supreme Court case called Hosanna-Tabor Evangelical Lutheran Church and School v. Equal Employment Opportunity Commission, which some observers have called the most important religious freedom case in 20 years.[8]

The ruling came on January 11, 2012. The Supreme Court ruled unanimously in favor of a church's right to define itself and its ministries and run its affairs accordingly, free from government interference in what constitutes a "minister".[9]

When the government's lawyer argued, months earlier, that there's no ministerial exception in the Constitution, only the same rights that secular organizations have to choose their own affiliations, Justice Antonin Scalia erupted. "That's extraordinary! There, black on white in the text of the Constitution, are special protections for religion. And you say it makes no difference?"[10]

Justice Elena Kagan agreed with Scalia's rejection of the argument that the First Amendment doesn't protect churches from government ordering who they should hire as pastor or priest. She called the government overreach "amazing".[11]

Just over a week after the final ruling, on January 19, 2012, Pope Benedict issued a message for the Church in the United States during a meeting with U.S. bishops. The letter, about the growing threat of radical secularism in America, was a warning.

[8] William P. Mumma, "Theology Up for Debate at SCOTUS?" *Washington Post*, National Section, Oct. 5, 2011, http://www.washingtonpost.com/blogs/guest-voices/post/theology-up-for-debate-at-scotus/2011/10/05/gIQAbIuVNL_blog.html.

[9] Supreme Court of the United States, *Hosanna-Tabor Evangelical Lutheran Church and School v. Equal Employment Opportunity Commission*, No. 10-553, decided Jan. 11, 2012, http://www.supremecourt.gov/opinions/11pdf/10-553.pdf.

[10] "Kagan Balks at Obama EEOC Claim of Authority over Churches", *Washington Examiner*, Oct. 5, 2011, http://washingtonexaminer.com/article/41157.

[11] Steve Chapman, "Surprising Truth to 'Obama's War on Religion'", *Washington Examiner*, Dec. 12, 2011, http://washingtonexaminer.com/article/156749.

> [I]t is imperative that the entire Catholic community in the United States come to realize the grave threats to the Church's public moral witness presented by a radical secularism which finds increasing expression in the political and cultural spheres. The seriousness of these threats needs to be clearly appreciated at every level of ecclesial life. Of particular concern are certain attempts being made to limit that most cherished of American freedoms, the freedom of religion. Many of you have pointed out that concerted efforts have been made to deny the right of conscientious objection on the part of Catholic individuals and institutions with regard to cooperation in intrinsically evil practices.[12]

The next day, on January 20, 2012, the Obama administration issued the HHS mandate. This was an extraordinary provocation.

On the day after Pope Benedict warned the Church in America about unprecedented political and cultural threats to religious freedom, the Obama administration issued a mandate that would force religious institutions to comply with health care rules profoundly against their fundamental moral beliefs.

The American Center for Law and Justice was already involved in lawsuits on the Obama health care legislation. "Never before has an American president so openly and wantonly disregarded the religious civil liberties of so many", said an ACLJ attorney.[13] The federal rule required that insurance policies provide for contraceptive services, including sterilization, and drugs that could induce abortions.

> With this rule, hundreds of religious colleges and hospitals, for example, will now be required—in fact, coerced—into providing insurance coverage for practices they believe to be morally wrong and violative of their religious beliefs. These institutions, which have educated citizens and cared for the infirm for hundreds of years, will now have to cave into the federal government or close their doors.[14]

U.S. bishops' conference president Timothy Cardinal Dolan, Archbishop of New York, responded in an op-ed piece in the *Wall Street Journal* and many of the nation's larger newspapers.

[12] Pope Benedict XVI, "Address of His Holiness Benedict XVI to the Bishops of the United States of America on their 'Ad Limina' Visit" (Jan. 19, 2012), http://www.vatican.va/holy_father/benedict_xvi/speeches/2012/january/documents/hf_ben-xvi_spe_20120119_bishops-usa_en.html.

[13] Geoffrey Surtees, "Religious Liberties Violated by Obama's Forced Coverage of Abortion Pills", American Center for Law and Justice, Jan. 23, 2012, http://aclj.org/obamacare/religious-liberties-violated-obama-forced-coverage-abortion-pills.

[14] Ibid.

> Religious freedom is the lifeblood of the American people, the cornerstone of American government. When the Founding Fathers determined that the innate rights of men and women should be enshrined in our Constitution, they so esteemed religious liberty that they made it the first freedom in the Bill of Rights.
>
> In particular, the Founding Fathers fiercely defended the right of conscience. George Washington himself declared: "The conscientious scruples of all men should be treated with great delicacy and tenderness; and it is my wish and desire, that the laws may always be extensively accommodated to them." James Madison, a key defender of religious freedom and author of the First Amendment, said: "Conscience is the most sacred of all property."[15]

Yet the Obama administration has veered in the opposite direction ... This was a radical departure from U.S. law and custom.

> Last August, when the administration first proposed this nationwide mandate for contraception and sterilization coverage, it also proposed a "religious employer" exemption. But this was so narrow that ... even Jesus and His disciples would not qualify for the exemption in that case, because they were committed to serve those of other faiths.
>
> Since then, hundreds of religious institutions, and hundreds of thousands of individual citizens, have raised their voices in principled opposition to this requirement that religious institutions and individuals violate their own basic moral teaching in their health plans. Certainly many of these good people and groups were Catholic, but many were Americans of other faiths, or no faith at all, who recognize that their beliefs could be next on the block. They also recognize that the cleverest way for the government to erode the broader principle of religious freedom is to target unpopular beliefs first.[16]

In one sweeping move, President Obama and his Catholic health secretary succeeded in something no other groups or efforts or initiatives or projects have been able to do: unite and galvanize Catholics on the right and left. The *Wall Street Journal* columnist William McGurn commented:

> Less predictable—and far more interesting—has been the heat from the Catholic left, including many who have in the past given the president

[15] Timothy M. Dolan, "ObamaCare and Religious Freedom: How about Some Respect for Catholics and Others Who Object to Treating Pregnancy as a Disease?" *Wall Street Journal*, Opinion, Jan. 25, 2012, http://blog.archny.org/images/2012/01/WSJ-ObamaCare-and-Religious-Freedom.pdf.

[16] Ibid.

> vital cover. In a post for the left-leaning *National Catholic Reporter*, Michael Sean Winters minces few words. Under the headline "J'ACCUSE," he rightly takes the president to the woodshed for the politics of the decision, for the substance, and for how "shamefully" it treats "those Catholics who went out on a limb" for him.
>
> The message Mr. Obama is sending, says Mr. Winters, is "that there is no room in this great country of ours for the institutions our Church has built over the years to be Catholic in ways that are important to us." ... Catholic liberals appreciate that this HHS decision is more than a return to the hostility that sent so many Catholic Democrats fleeing to the Republican Party these past few decades. They understand that if left to stand, this ruling threatens the religious institutions closest to their hearts—those serving Americans in need, such as hospitals, soup kitchens and immigrant services.[17]

What concerned so many people on both the left and right at the time, and continues to concern them, is that government will step in and assume the role of provider in place of the great tradition of Christian social ministry. The *New York Times* columnist Ross Douthat called the president's move a particularly cruel betrayal of the Catholic Democrats who helped elect him and now "find that their government's communitarianism leaves no room for their church's communitarianism, and threatens to regulate it out of existence".[18]

> When government expands, it's often at the expense of alternative expressions of community, alternative groups that seek to serve the common good. Unlike most communal organizations, the government has coercive power—the power to regulate, to mandate and to tax. These advantages make it all too easy for the state to gradually crowd out its rivals....
>
> Sometimes this crowding out happens gradually, subtly, indirectly. Every tax dollar the government takes is a dollar that can't go to charities and churches. Every program the government runs, from education to health care to the welfare office, can easily become a kind of taxpayer-backed monopoly.

[17] William McGurn, "Obama Offends the Catholic Left: A Contraceptive Mandate Provokes an Unnecessary War", *Wall Street Journal*, Opinion: Main Street, Jan. 24, 2012, http://online.wsj.com/article/SB10001424052970203718504577179110264196498.html.

[18] Ross Douthat, "Government and Its Rivals", *New York Times*, Sunday Review, Opinion Pages, Jan. 28, 2012, http://www.nytimes.com/2012/01/29/opinion/sunday/douthat-government-and-its-rivals.html.

> But sometimes the state goes further. Not content with crowding out alternative forms of common effort, it presents its rivals an impossible choice: Play by our rules, even if it means violating the moral ideals that inspired your efforts in the first place, or get out of the community-building business entirely.[19]

No, say Catholic bishops and other religious leaders. The Rev. Dr. Matthew Harrison, president of the Lutheran Church–Missouri Synod, testified before a House Committee on the mandate in March 2012. "Religious people determine what violates their consciences, not the federal government. The conscience is a sacred thing. Our church exists because overzealous governments in northern Europe made decisions which trampled the religious convictions of our forbearers."[20]

Abraham Lincoln stood up for the cause of religious freedom in the 1840s and particularly on behalf of Catholics, regarded and treated by the Nativists with hostility. At a meeting he organized in Springfield, Illinois, on June 12, 1844, Lincoln proposed the following resolution: That "the guarantee of the rights of conscience, as found in our Constitution, is most sacred and inviolable, and one that belongs no less to the Catholic, than to the Protestant, and that all attempts to abridge or interfere with these rights, either of Catholic or Protestant, directly or indirectly, have our decided disapprobation, and shall ever have our most effective opposition."[21]

## First among Freedoms

Christians have faced intolerance and persecution across the world throughout history and do today. Many are under threat of violence just for being Christians, or for being known openly to hold Christian beliefs and act on them in a public way, according to their morally informed consciences. In this country, we've had a constitutionally protected right to hold and act on our beliefs through the religious freedom guaranteed in the First Amendment. In fact, when the Constitution

[19] Ibid.

[20] "Missouri Synod President Tells House Committee: LCMS 'Religiously Opposed to Supporting Abortion-Causing Drugs'", Lutheran Church Missouri Synod, Feb. 16, 2012, http://www.lcms.org/page.aspx?pid=1374.

[21] J. G. Nicolay and John Hay, "Lincoln, Abraham: A History", *Century Illustrated Monthly Magazine: The Making of America Project*, vol. 33 (New York: Century Co., 1887), p. 396.

was first drafted, the people of this young country wanted more protection of basic rights and liberties. So the First Congress proposed a Bill of Rights, which became the first ten amendments to the U.S. Constitution.

Ordering them was an act of honoring the highest priorities of a nation of people who wanted to be just and good and have the principles in which they believed protected foremost. So the First Amendment begins with religious freedom, and both of its twofold protections go together and must not be separated. First Amendment religious freedom protection both prohibits an official, government-sponsored religion ("*Congress shall make no law respecting an establishment of religion* ...") and protects the people in their free exercise of religion ("... *or prohibiting the free exercise thereof*").[22] That means citizens can privately and publicly practice their religion by expressing their beliefs and acting on them in ways they see as moral and rejecting what they believe is immoral. The government cannot compel or coerce them to be complicit in any action people believe to be immoral.

That has been upheld over time and reinforced with the Religious Freedom Restoration Act of 1993, a federal law with bipartisan support in Congress that added another layer of protection from government infringement on religious liberty. RFRA, as it is known, prevents laws that substantially burden people's free exercise of their religion.

In RFRA, Congress states, "Government shall not substantially burden a person's exercise of religion even if the burden results from a rule of general applicability".[23] The key to its strength is in setting the bar very high for any government attempt to test it through two parts, and both conditions must be met to allow for any exception to the law. First, *the government must prove it has a compelling interest which necessitates a law* that burdens a person's exercise of religion, and what suffices as "compelling interest" relates directly with core constitutional issues. The second condition is that the rule or *law must be the least restrictive way in which to further the government interest.*

What the government did in early 2012 by issuing the HHS mandate cannot stand the test of that application. Asma Uddin, a Becket Fund for

[22] U.S. Constitution Bill of Rights (emphasis added).

[23] *Religious Freedom Restoration Act of 1993*, Pub. L. No. 103–41, 107 Stat. 1488 (Nov. 16, 1993), 42 U.S.C. §2000bb–1(a), http://www.gpo.gov/fdsys/pkg/USCODE-2009-title42/html/USCODE-2009-title42-chap21B.htm.

Religious Liberty attorney who specializes in domestic and international religious liberty cases, gave testimony before a House Judiciary Committee soon after the mandate was issued and Becket was called upon to challenge it in a number of court cases across the country. Uddin walked legislators clearly through a well-reasoned argument.

> The HHS mandate is not only unprecedented in federal law, but also broader in scope and narrower in its exemption than all ... comparable laws....
>
> These lawsuits challenge the government Mandate as a violation of the First Amendment of the U.S. Constitution, the Religious Freedom Restoration Act (RFRA), and the Administrative Procedures Act (APA). The religious freedom claims turn on the fact that the burden placed on these organizations is not justified, as is required by law, by a compelling government interest that is narrowly tailored to serve that interest....
>
> Some have framed the controversy surrounding the Mandate as a women's rights issue. At the outset, the point must be made that our clients are acting because of what is being asked for (an act that violates their deeply held beliefs), rather than who is doing the asking.[24]

This testimony clears the smoke screen that covered underlying issues behind the mandate in the first place, which very few major media did in their coverage. They perpetuated the "women's rights" theme, which is a socially constructed ideology, and left aside factual evidence. Uddin brought that to the hearing.

> Moreover, including a robust exemption protecting the deeply held religious beliefs of those who oppose contraception and abortion would not harm women or women's health. Access to these contraceptives is widespread: Nine out of ten employer-based insurance plans in the United States already cover contraception. The government admits these services are widely available in "community health centers, public clinics, and hospitals with income-based support."
>
> *In fact, the federal government already spends hundreds of millions of dollars each year funding free or nearly free family planning services under its Title X program. Therefore, the issue is not really about access to contraception but rather about who pays for it.*[25]

[24] "Testimony of Asma T. Uddin on behalf of The Becket Fund for Religious Liberty", U.S. House of Representatives Committee on the Judiciary (Feb. 28, 2012), pp. 4, 7, http://judiciary.house.gov/hearings/Hearings%202012/Uddin%2002282012.pdf.

[25] Ibid. (emphasis added).

She concluded with a powerful point.

> Finally, one of the issues that is consistently overlooked when the issue is framed as "women's rights versus religious freedom" is that women, too, seek the freedom to live in accordance with their sincerely held religious beliefs.... As a female member of [a] religious minority, I hold this right to religious freedom particularly dear, as, for example, a Muslim woman's right to dress as she pleases is restricted by many governments across the world.[26]

Asma Uddin is a Muslim woman attorney working for the Becket Fund for Religious Liberty. That firm has been fighting for religious freedom rights for people of different beliefs throughout the world for many years.

They probably saw this coming, because some scholars, journalists, and religious leaders did. In June 2010, the *Washington Post* religion blog posted a lengthy commentary by former American diplomat Thomas F. Farr, then Visiting Associate Professor of Religion and World Affairs and Senior Fellow at the Berkley Center for Religion, Peace, and World Affairs. Its title was a question, expressing his concern: "National Security without Religious Liberty?"

He said pursuing international religious freedom is a national security matter, and he feared President Obama was putting it "on the back burner, subordinating it to other less compelling administration priorities, or clearing the deck for initiatives that might be complicated by a robust defense of religious liberty abroad (such as outreach to Muslim majority countries or promoting international gay rights)."[27]

> The 1998 International Religious Freedom Act, passed unanimously by Congress, was signed into law by President Bill Clinton. It was implemented in the early stages by Secretary Madeleine Albright, who has since written a book calling for greater attention to religion in American foreign policy....
>
> Both history and contemporary scholarship demonstrate that democracy cannot remain stable, or yield its benefits to all citizens, without religious freedom. The absence of religious liberty in a highly religious

[26] Ibid.

[27] Thomas Farr, "National Security without Religious Liberty?" *Washington Post*, On Faith, June 7, 2010, http://newsweek.washingtonpost.com/onfaith/georgetown/2010/06/a_national_security_strategy_without_religious_freedom.html.

society leads to violence, extremism and, in some cases, religion-based terrorism, including the kind that has been exported to American shores.[28]

This is incisive, important analysis.

In March, the bipartisan House IRF [international religious freedom] caucus told the President that promoting religious freedom "will lead to greater human freedom, economic prosperity and security throughout the world."

The same month a bipartisan group of scholars and human rights experts organized by Freedom House was even more explicit. They urged the President to "articulate concrete connections and synergies ... between religious freedom policy and other key foreign policy areas, including national security....

In May the U.S. Commission on International Religious Freedom's annual report joined the chorus: "religious freedom should be increasingly more important as one of the core considerations in foreign policy and national security."[29]

Farr was concerned, very concerned, that at that point the administration in office was ignoring such an important concern for human rights and national security in spite of all this urging.

[T]he new strategy simply ignores growing evidence that, in most countries of the world, none of these objectives is achievable without a robust regime of religious liberty.

But it gets worse. The National Security Strategy contains a five-page section entitled "Values." It begins as follows, "The United States believes certain values are universal and will work to promote them worldwide." Those values include democracy, human rights, and human dignity.

It seems unimaginable that any group of American officials—even the most secular minded realists—could pen five pages on American values, and how they might contribute to our security in a highly religious world, without significant attention to religious liberty. Our own history demonstrates that neither democracy, [nor] human rights, nor human dignity can be sustained without religious liberty.[30]

That is powerful affirmation of what has historically been conclusive.

[28] Ibid.
[29] Ibid.
[30] Ibid.

But Farr wasn't finished yet.

> It turns out that the list of the most important American values includes things like ensuring transparency, refraining from torture, protecting privacy, and "promoting the right to access information."
>
> But not religious freedom.
>
> The only hint of religious liberty in this section comes in a single reference to "an individual's freedom ... to worship as they please." This is thin (and ungrammatical) tokenism. Not only is the phrase a brief, almost throw-away aside in an extended analysis of ostensibly universal American values, but the very concept of "individual freedom of worship" represents an impoverished understanding of religious liberty.[31]

This has been a key point for the Obama administration, but one that has missed the radar of most media. Farr makes that point in delivering his strong conclusion, one that calls for attention. Note this and follow closely:

> One prominent American intellectual has put the issue this way:
>
> "[S]ecularists are wrong when they ask believers to leave their religion at the door before entering into the public square. Frederick Douglas, Abraham Lincoln, Williams Jennings Bryan, Dorothy Day, Martin Luther King—indeed, the majority of great reformers in American history—were not only motivated by faith, but repeatedly used religious language to argue for their cause. So to say that men and women should not inject their 'personal morality' into public policy debates is a practical absurdity. Our law is by definition a codification of morality, much of it grounded in the Judeo-Christian tradition."
>
> That intellectual was Barack Obama in his 2008 Call to Renewal speech. A year later, as President, he told a Muslim audience in Cairo that "freedom of religion is central to the ability of peoples to live together" and named religious freedom a key issue to be addressed by Muslim majority countries. Judged by his words, no President has had a more vigorous understanding of the meaning and reach of religious liberty in the lives of human beings and societies.
>
> Rarely have word and deed been so estranged.[32]

That became all the more evident in the years after Farr wrote that commentary.[33] But around that same time, others were noticing the

[31] Ibid.

[32] Ibid.

[33] Interestingly, the Obama speech Farr quotes has been removed from Obama's blog since the publication of Farr's article in 2010.

president or members of his administration were using the phrase "freedom of worship" instead of "freedom of religion", and it's more than semantics. There's a big difference between those two freedoms. Just before Independence Day weekend 2010, the Chuck Colson Center for Christian Worldview sent out an alert about the redefinition of religious freedom that was possibly happening in American government.[34] *Christianity Today* also noticed and published an article saying that the Obama administration was using the terms interchangeably, as if they were equivalent.[35] They're not.

Nina Shea, director of the Center for Religious Freedom and a member of the U.S. Commission on International Religious Freedom, told *Christianity Today* that "freedom of worship" means the right to pray within a place of worship, or privately to hold religious beliefs. "It excludes the right to raise your children in your faith; the right to have religious literature; the right to meet with co-religionists; the right to raise funds; the right to appoint or elect your religious leaders, and to carry out charitable activities, to evangelize, [and] to have religious education or seminary training", she clarified.[36]

When the challenges to religious freedom mounted throughout 2011 and then reached the beginning of 2012 when the HHS mandate raised that threat level, the U.S. Conference of Catholic Bishops published an eloquent document called *Our First, Most Cherished Liberty*. In it, they address this issue under a section subheaded "Religious Liberty Is More Than Freedom of Worship".

> It is about whether we can make our contribution to the common good of all Americans. Can we do the good works our faith calls us to do, without having to compromise that very same faith? Without religious liberty properly understood, all Americans suffer, deprived of the essential contribution in education, health care, feeding the hungry, civil rights, and social services that religious Americans make every day, both here at home and overseas.

[34] Chuck Colson, "Freedom of Worship: An Anorexic Description of Our Rights", Chuck Colson Center for Christian Worldview, June 30, 2010, http://www.colsoncenter.org/the-center/the-chuck-colson-center/two-minute-warning/15391-freedom-of-worship-chuck-colson.

[35] Sarah Eekhoff Zylstra, "'Freedom of Worship' Worries: New Religious Freedom Rhetoric within the Obama Administration Draws Concern", *Christianity Today*, June 22, 2010, http://www.christianitytoday.com/ct/2010/july/2.12.html.

[36] Ibid.

What is at stake is whether America will continue to have a free, creative, and robust civil society—or whether the state alone will determine who gets to contribute to the common good, and how they get to do it. Religious believers are part of American civil society, which includes neighbors helping each other, community associations, fraternal service clubs, sports leagues, and youth groups. All these Americans make their contribution to our common life, and they do not need the permission of the government to do so. Restrictions on religious liberty are an attack on civil society and the American genius for voluntary associations.

The Union of Orthodox Jewish Congregations of America issued a statement about the administration's contraception and sterilization mandate that captured exactly the danger that we face.

This is not a Catholic issue. This is not a Jewish issue. This is not an Orthodox, Mormon, or Muslim issue. It is an American issue.[37]

## Conscience Rights and Natural Law

The human right to conscience is not just a great American tradition; it preexists the State and every other conceivable form of government since it comes from God. Those who deny there even is such a thing as "natural law" or rights conferred by the Creator or a moral code written on the human heart don't eliminate what they refuse to accept. They just play by different rules.

How do you engage people like that?

Here's an interesting thought experiment. In Vatican observer Sandro Magister's "The Deafening Silence of Pope Karol Wojtyla", two professors discuss the thought of John Paul II on the natural law as the limit governments must never transgress. John Paul stated that abortion laws are "the most terrible product of totalitarianism disguised as democracy", and called them "lacking in legal validity".[38] The setup question is this: "Can the life and death of a human being be decided by a majority?" Professor Giovanni Sartori claims: "The decision a mother makes to abort is not by majority, it is individual. The majority simply votes on the laws that allow this choice.... There are rules on this point that have been decided by majority, by a democratically elected parliament.

[37] USCCB, "Religious Liberty Is More Than Freedom of Worship", *Our First, Most Cherished Liberty: A Statement on Religious Liberty* (Apr. 12, 2012), http://www.usccb.org/issues-and-action/religious-liberty/our-first-most-cherished-liberty.cfm.

[38] Sandro Magister, "The Deafening Silence of Pope Karol Wojtyla", www.chiesa, Mar. 3, 2005, http://chiesa.espresso.repubblica.it/articolo/24160?eng=y.

But these rules do not say to the individual: you must do this. They say: If you wish, it is your right to do this."[39]

Similarly, Roman philosopher and accomplished professor Dario Antiseri publicly and extensively criticized Pope Benedict's fundamental message of the "new humanism", discounting even its premise that people are essentially spiritual, in search of truth and God, informed by the "law written on the heart". Furthermore, Antiseri actually defends relativism and even nihilism, and he rejects outright the ability of the "natural law" belief to withstand the test of reason. He argues on behalf of "those who maintain that any ethical system is as good as another, that all ethical systems are the same, that nothing is worthwhile—or rather that no value is truly valid".[40]

Antiseri argues for a pluralism of ethics, saying the inevitable question is "[D]o we have available to us a rational criterion, one that is valid for all, according to which we can decide which ethics is best in that it is rationally founded?" And further, "the *fundamental ethical principles* ... are in the final analysis founded upon *each person's choices of conscience*, and not on arguments of a rational nature".[41]

What would we say to that?

Benedict's answer can be found in a very interesting lecture "Conscience in Its Time", one of many assembled in his book *Church, Ecumenism, and Politics*. Benedict says:

> In his memoirs, *Conversations with Hitler*, Hermann Rauschning ... reports the following remark made by the dictator to him: "I liberate man from the coercion of a mind that has become an end in itself; from the dirty and degrading self-inflicted torments of a chimera called conscience and morality and from the demands of a freedom and personal autonomy to which only a very few can ever measure up."[42]

Benedict responds:

> The destruction of the conscience is the real prerequisite for totalitarian followers and totalitarian rule. Where conscience prevails, there is

[39] Ibid.

[40] Dario Antiseri, "A Spy in the Service of the Most High", *Vita e Pensiero*, cited in Sandro Magister, "Disputed Questions: A Catholic Philosopher Argues for Relativism", www.Chiesa, Nov. 30, 2005, http://chiesa.espresso.repubblica.it/articolo/41533?eng=y.

[41] Ibid. (emphasis added).

[42] Joseph Cardinal Ratzinger, "Conscience in Its Time", in *Church, Ecumenism, and Politics: New Endeavors in Ecclesiology* (San Francisco: Ignatius Press, 2008), p. 160.

> a limit to the dominion of human command and human choice, something sacred that must remain inviolate and that in its ultimate sovereignty eludes all control, whether someone else's or one's own. Only ... the recognition that conscience is sacrosanct protects man from man's inhumanity and from himself; only its rule guarantees freedom.[43]

That is powerful.

For those who don't immediately access Benedict's profoundly elegant teaching of the human person, how are they to answer the cultural tide toward widespread abortion on demand as private choice, euthanasia as compassion, embryonic stem cell research as scientific hope, homosexual marriage as human rights, and "diversity and tolerance" education purged of religion as enlightenment for the common good?

Princeton Professor Robert George has answers, plenty of them found in his excellent book *The Clash of Orthodoxies: Law, Religion and Morality in Crisis*.[44] And he had an answer for Sartori's point that a law that allows abortion doesn't compel it—a point made by Catholic American politicians in the position "I'm personally opposed but want to keep it legal"—a position we hear often and a response George often makes.

> There is, they insist, no problem in remaining faithful to the Church's teaching on the sanctity of unborn human life, while at the same time honoring what they take to be a necessary freedom in pluralistic democratic societies. The fallacy at the heart of their argument is, however, glaring.
>
> The question is not whether it is psychologically possible for a legislator to will that women have a choice as to whether to have abortions while hoping that they never choose that option. The problem for pro-choice Catholics is that it is impossible to will that women have the freedom to abort without at the same time willing that the unborn as a class be denied the elementary and fundamental legal protections against being killed that all of us desire and support for ourselves and others whose lives we believe are worthy of the law's protection.[45]

We need to simplify this.

[43] Ibid.

[44] Robert P. George, *The Clash of Orthodoxies: Law, Religion and Morality in Crisis* (Wilmington, Del.: ISI Books, 2001).

[45] "Princeton's Robert George on Reasonableness of Christian Morality: Tells Why Moral Principles Outdo Secularist Ideologies", *Zenit*, Jan. 10, 2002, http://www.zenit.org/en/articles/princeton-s-robert-george-on-reasonableness-of-christian-morality.

## Clearly Defining Terms

Archbishop Joseph Naumann confronted the nonsense of rhetoric being used in public debate to cover for what is really being said behind politically crafted language. In a talk he gave at the *Gospel of Life* conference in 2007 and posted soon after as an article at *First Things* online magazine titled "Woe to Those Who Call Evil Good", Naumann called on people to speak clearly, ask questions, and follow ideas through to their logical conclusions.

> It is the crisis of truth that allows otherwise intelligent individuals to posit that they are personally opposed to abortion, but they support the right of others to choose an abortion.
>
> The question that needs to be posed to those who make this claim is: Why are you personally opposed to abortion? Why do so many of the pro-choice politicians even say that they want to make abortion rare? Why want to make something rare if it is truly a valid choice? The rhetoric of choice has been a very clever marketing campaign for something that is of its nature evil and repugnant.
>
> While it taps into some deeply held American values of personal freedom and individual liberty, [the] pro-choice position is actually an exercise in illogic. Nobody is actually pro-choice in the sense that they are in favor of all choices. Indeed, one always has to ask the further question: What is being chosen? In the case of abortion, the honest answer is: to destroy a human life....
>
> Without the acceptance of objective truth, everything becomes negotiable.[46]

How do pro-life politicians or political activists turn "pro-choice?" Senator Ted Kennedy was once staunchly pro-life. In an opinion piece in the *Wall Street Journal* in January 2009, author Anne Henderschott recalls the senator's pro-life stance:

> In fact, in 1971, a full year after New York had legalized abortion, the Massachusetts senator was still championing the rights of the unborn. In a letter to a constituent dated Aug. 3, 1971, he wrote: "When history looks back to this era it should recognize this generation as one which cared about human beings enough to halt the practice of war, to provide a

[46]Joseph Naumann, "Woe to Those Who Call Evil Good", *First Things*, Oct. 29, 2007, http://www.firstthings.com/onthesquare/2007/10/woe-to-those-who-call-evil-goo.

decent living for every family, and to fulfill its responsibility to its children from the very moment of conception."[47]

Rev. Jesse Jackson is another example. In *Right to Life News*, January 1977 edition, Jesse Jackson wrote an article titled "How We Respect Life Is the Over-Riding Moral Issue". Here's how he begins: "The question of 'life' is *The Question* of the 20th century. Race and poverty are dimensions of the life question, but discussions about abortion have brought the issue into focus in a much sharper way. How we will respect and understand the nature of life itself is the over-riding moral issue, not of the Black race, but of the human race."[48]

Rev. Dr. Martin Luther King, Jr., was not a politician and never wavered from his activism on behalf of human rights, dignity, equality, and justice "for all God's children", reflecting in his sermons, speeches, and writing the understanding that achieving those goals required obedience to God's law, witnessing to truth found in the Scriptures, and calling others to recognize these truths, come what may.

Two writers make a point of King's public witness to faith as the formation of a just society in their article "MLK's Philosophical and Theological Legacy", published in *Public Discourse.* "Those who praise the modern civil rights movement, but who also want to keep morality and theology absent from public discourse, seldom mention King's reliance on natural law in his justly famous letter [Letter from Birmingham Jail]", says Justin Dyer, and he notes, "and his defense of civil disobedience drew from the work of Thomas Aquinas in particular."[49]

> King was, first and foremost, a pastor, nurtured in the Christian tradition and sharpened by his encounter with the classic texts of Western philosophy. His description of segregation ordinances as "morally wrong and sinful" occurred within a theological framework....
>
> These aspects of King's letter provide a challenge to modern theorists who would, as a matter of principle, scrub the public sphere clean of all philosophy and theology. Lest their insistence on a naked public square appear to be merely an unprincipled attempt to silence conservative moral

[47] Anne Henderschott, "How Support for Abortion Became Kennedy Dogma", *Wall Street Journal*, Jan. 2, 2009.

[48] Jesse Jackson, "How We Respect Life Is the Over-Riding Moral Issue", *Right to Life News*, Jan. 1977.

[49] Justin Dyer, "MLK's Philosophical and Theological Legacy", *The Witherspoon Institute: Public Discourse*, Jan. 16, 2012, http://www.thepublicdiscourse.com/2012/01/4503.

> and religious arguments, they must reluctantly exclude much of King, as well. Attempts to erase or diminish King's theological and philosophical commitments will not do, for although he was famous for declaring that he had a dream, we sometimes forget that his dream was of a world in which "every valley shall be exalted, and every hill and mountain shall be made low, the rough places will be made plain, and the crooked places will be made straight." One of the most famous passages of King's most famous political speech comes verbatim from the fortieth chapter of the book of Isaiah, and the original context was a prophetic vision of one preparing the way for the political rule of God.[50]

As noted earlier, Pope John XXIII issued his Encyclical *Pacem in Terris* in this same period of time in 1963, and he cited the same part of Thomas Aquinas' teaching on just law and moral order to show that they come from God. Pope John contrasted the order in the universe with the disorder and disunity among individuals and nations in the world.

> One would think that the relationships that bind men together could only be governed by force.
>
> But the world's Creator has stamped man's inmost being with an order revealed to man by his conscience; and his conscience insists on his preserving it. Men "show the work of the law written in their hearts. Their conscience bears witness to them." And how could it be otherwise? All created being reflects the infinite wisdom of God....
>
> *But the mischief is often caused by erroneous opinions.* Many people think that the laws which govern man's relations with the State are the same as those which regulate the blind, elemental forces of the universe. But it is not so; *the laws which govern men are quite different. The Father of the universe has inscribed them in man's nature, and that is where we must look for them; there and nowhere else.*
>
> These laws clearly indicate how a man must behave toward his fellows in society, and how the mutual relationships between the members of a State and its officials are to be conducted. They show too what principles must govern the relations between States; and finally, what should be the relations between individuals or States on the one hand, and the world-wide community of nations on the other.[51]

This was the pope who convened the Second Vatican Council to open the Church to the modern world and send the laity out to engage it in

[50] Ibid.

[51] Pope John XXIII, *Pacem in Terris* (Apr. 11, 1963), no. 51 (emphasis added).

new ways, believing that peace in the world can only come through order, and that only comes through a morally informed core of beliefs.

And now we're in a critical and challenging time when morally informed voices are being driven out of the public square and threatened in new ways from the freedom of expression. The erosion of freedoms calls for the strongest of defense, and the Catholic Church and Christians and people of other religions in solidarity with them have met the threats to our freedoms with renewed activism.

## The Church as Bulwark

"This brings us to the most grievous moral and constitutional failing of the administration's latest gambit. It presumes that the government has the power to say who has any religious freedom, and how much", says Matthew Franck in his article written for *Public Discourse*.[52] The Obama administration had just announced what was claimed as a "compromise" to its contraceptive mandate that violates religious freedom and conscience rights.

Franck claimed that

> even the non-religious—though lacking a claim defensible under the First Amendment's protection of religious freedom—are capable of stating a conscientious moral objection to the government's command that they commit a wrong or pay a penalty, which is one reason why the Catholic bishops have insisted from the first that the only "exemption" worth discussing is a wholesale rescission of the HHS mandate....
>
> ... The administration has *conceded* that religious freedom is at stake in the struggle over its mandate, but it has dictated for whom that freedom exists, when it is truly the common possession of all....
>
> If that seems to you like an alarmist reaction to the administration's reassurance, ask yourself this. Given its stated hostility to any serious understanding of our first freedom, the right not just to worship but to live one's faith in all one's daily work, on what understanding of our remaining constitutional freedoms can the administration assure us that any of these other liberties still stands on a firm foundation?[53]

[52] Matthew J. Franck, "Deciding Who Gets Religious Freedom: The Latest HHS 'Accommodation'", *The Witherspoon Institute: Public Discourse*, Feb. 7, 2013, http://www.thepublicdiscourse.com/2013/02/7883.

[53] Ibid.

Chicago's Cardinal Francis George wrote a column in the Archdiocese of Chicago's *Catholic New World* entitled "Conscience", published October 23, 2011, when the "window for public comment" on the HHS rules was closed and its mandate imminent.

> Already the outreach of Catholic Charities in this and other states has been curtailed by a change in the marriage laws. In all these instances, those protesting government intrusions on conscience appeal to long-established American civil law: The state has no right to coerce conscience, whether personal or institutional, nor to define what a religious ministry should look like. What is at stake in this public conversation? What is at stake, first of all, is religious freedom....
>
> What is also at stake is personal freedom to act publicly on the basis of one's religious faith.... What history teaches clearly, however, is that when the dominant culture and its laws eliminate religious freedom, the state becomes sacred. No appeal to God or to a morality based on religious faith is allowed to break into the closed circle of civil legalism. The state's coercive power is not limited to keeping external order; it invades the internal realm of one's relation to God. The state becomes a church.[54]

The events covered here so far have pointed to a consequential transformation in that direction in recent years. There are others worth noting, as Ken Blackwell, former U.S. Ambassador to the U.N. Human Rights Commission, did in his letter to General Colin Powell (cited earlier) and published on Townhall.com, January 14, 2013.[55] Already cited earlier here was his concern that the delegates and officials at the 2012 Democratic National Convention in Charlotte, North Carolina, nearly left God out of the party platform, and that a voice vote repeated three times called for that removal.

A single voice, the voice of a narrator, made a statement on a brief opening video presentation at that convention that caused a stir among some political commentators. "We believe you can use government in a good way", the narrator said. "*Government is the only thing we all belong to*. We have different churches, different clubs, but we're together as a

[54] Francis Cardinal George, O.M.I., "Conscience", *Catholic New World*, Oct. 23, 2011, http://www.catholicnewworld.com/cnwonline/2011/1023/cardinal.aspx.

[55] Ken Blackwell, "Who Are the Intolerant? Ken Blackwell Writes an Open Letter to General Powell", Jan. 15, 2013, article provided by Townhall, http://townhall.com/columnists/kenblackwell/2013/01/14/an-open-letter-to-general-powell-n1488741/page/full.

part of our city, or our county, or our state and our nation."[56] That is not a traditionally American view of the role of government in the lives of its citizens. But this is not the traditional Democratic Party any longer.

Blackwell is one of many public voices who lament that fact, and he expressed it in his open letter.

> What has happened to the Democratic Party that, in the 1960s, provided such leadership for the cause of Civil Rights? It was Democrats like John F. Kennedy and Hubert Humphrey who supported the fight for civil rights among the white majority in the 1960s. Kennedy, the first Catholic president, was in good company in his church.
>
> Roman Catholic Bishops were among the first to strike out against segregation in the 1950s and 1960s. The Rev. Dr. Martin Luther King, Jr., was surely a Baptist preacher, but he could rely on thousands of Catholic priests and nuns to join his great March on Washington in 1963....
>
> For the Democratic Party of Kennedy and King to vote three times to reject God was a shock to millions of black Americans. And it must have been especially shocking to black clergymen who have been leaders in the struggle for equal rights and equal opportunity for four decades and more. It is bad enough these pastors and their congregations have been given short shrift by the new elites in the Democratic Party, but we now see that God was not put in the back of the bus. God was not allowed on the bus at all....
>
> How far we have fallen from that great Inauguration Day in 1961 when John F. Kennedy said: "The rights of man come not from the generosity of the state, but from the hand of God." No one in America yelled NO! on that crisp, clear day in Washington....
>
> After slavery, after Jim Crow, after the KKK, it is fair to say that among the worst things visited upon black Americans have been the targeting of our families by abortionists and the effort to end marriage.
>
> That is why we are in a crisis. This is what happens when a major party rejects God.[57]

In his book *Render Unto Caesar*, Archbishop Charles Chaput warns about the tendencies of any politicians in any party to devalue religiously informed voices who speak out constantly about the truth, protection, and dignity of men.

[56] "Government Is the Only Thing We All Belong To", *BuzzFeed Politics*, Sept. 4, 2012, http://www.buzzfeed.com/buzzfeedpolitics/government-is-the-only-thing-we-all-belong-to (emphasis added).

[57] Blackwell, "Who Are the Intolerant?"

> The softer brand of God-aversion takes a different approach. It rewrites history, subtly uses fear.... The claims go like this.... A pluralistic society can't afford a dominant idea of God. Religious belief is too diverse. To avoid sectarian warfare, we need to keep religion out of the national public conversation. The state stands above moral and religious tribalism. It can best ensure the rights of everyone.[58]

We have been warned before, Chaput notes.

> The Christian scholar C.S. Lewis once famously warned of the "abolition of man"—that is, the destruction of what makes human beings "human"—by a scientific and technological elite. [B.F.] Skinner was well aware of Lewis's argument, and he specifically answered Lewis in *Beyond Freedom and Dignity* with the words: "To man *qua* man, we readily say good riddance. Only by dispossessing him can we turn to the real causes of human behavior. Only then can we turn from the inferred to the observed, from the miraculous to the natural, from the inaccessible to the *manipulable* [my italics]."
>
> This kind of knowledge-class bigotry amounts to barbarism with a graduate degree. As the great Protestant theologian Reinhold Niebuhr once said, "A barbarism developed in the heart of civilization has one important advantage over genuinely primitive barbarisms. It avails itself of all the technical advantages of civilization."[59]

One of these advantages is the modern communications media. Going back to Edmund Gettier's famous and highly consequential challenge to "the knowledge-class", how do they know what they know? And how do they justify it as true knowledge? We have to learn to ask the right questions and be prepared to follow through, in the great Catholic intellectual tradition, with a reasoned case for truth.

## Let's Be Clear:

1. **Everybody is born with a conscience and has the right and duty to form it well.** It is a sacred place of encounter between God and the soul. "Deep within his conscience man discovers a law which he has not laid upon himself but which he must obey. Its voice, ever

[58] Charles J. Chaput, *Render Unto Caesar: Serving the Nation by Living Our Catholic Beliefs in Political Life* (New York: Doubleday Religion, 2008), p. 27.

[59] Ibid., p. 26.

calling him to love and to do what is good and to avoid evil, sounds in his heart at the right moment."[60] A well-formed conscience is morally binding on the individual in all the dimensions of his moral, personal, and civic life. "Conscience must be informed and moral judgment enlightened. A well-formed conscience is upright and truthful. It formulates its judgments according to reason, in conformity with the true good willed by the wisdom of the Creator."[61]

2. **The Constitution guaranteed our "freedom of religion" not only a "freedom of worship".** The difference in terms is crucially important. *Religion* involves the totality of beliefs and convictions about how the individual should act in relation to God and others. *Worship* is limited to one type of action, usually liturgical in nature. We are free not only to express our beliefs in the walls of a church or other house of worship, but in every other way we express ourselves in society. Archbishop William Lori explains:

> While religious freedom certainly includes freedom of worship, it also includes the freedom of persons to live out their faith whatever their role in society—in social service ministries and in the marketplace, in the culture and in the public square. Religious beliefs that shape our entire lives, both inside and outside the sanctuary, have been the cornerstone of so many monumental causes—from the abolition of slavery, to women's suffrage, to the civil rights movement. While the voice of the Rev. Martin Luther King Jr. rang out from the pulpit of Ebenezer Baptist Church, it also rang out in the streets of Birmingham and Selma and Washington, D.C. True religious freedom includes the freedom to proclaim and practice religious faith, not just in private but in public as well.[62]

3. **Everyone holds moral principles and is guided by them.** Even the conviction that nobody should hold principles prescinding from organized religion (i.e., secularism) is itself a moral principle, one with which a person of faith would strongly disagree.

[60] Second Vatican Council, *Gaudium et Spes* (1965), no. 16; cf. *Catechism of the Catholic Church,* no. 1776.

[61] *Catechism of the Catholic Church,* no. 1783.

[62] Archbishop William Lori, "Beyond Fortnight: Emerging Challenges to Religious Freedom in the United States", *America,* July 1–8, 2013, http://americamagazine.org/issue/beyond-fortnight.

4. **Nobody has the right to force another person to violate his conscience.** Doing so would be the very epitome of coercion, and it would betray the very foundation of our founding documents. This is the tactic of totalitarian governments, against which the Church has always stood as a strong witness to the freedom of the individual. Vatican II declared that

> the human person has a right to religious freedom. This freedom means that all men are to be immune from coercion on the part of individuals or of social groups and of any human power, in such wise that no one is to be forced to act in a manner contrary to his own beliefs.... This right of the human person to religious freedom is to be recognized in the constitutional law whereby society is governed and thus it is to become a civil right.[63]

5. **Freedom must be ordered to truth.** Pope John Paul II declared:

> Freedom negates and destroys itself, and becomes a factor leading to the destruction of others, when it no longer recognizes and respects its essential link with the truth.... This view of freedom leads to a serious distortion of life in society.... In this way, any reference to common values and to a truth absolutely binding on everyone is lost, and social life ventures on to the shifting sands of complete relativism. At that point, *everything is negotiable*, everything is open to bargaining: even the first of the fundamental rights, the right to life.[64]

Over a decade later, Archbishop Joseph Naumann likewise stated: "Without the acceptance of objective truth, *everything becomes negotiable*."[65]

[63] Second Vatican Council, *Dignitatis Humanae* (1965), no. 2.
[64] Pope John Paul II, *Evangelium Vitae* (1995), nos. 19–20 (emphasis added).
[65] Naumann, "Woe to Those Who Call Evil Good" (emphasis added).

# Chapter 6

# Fighting for Dignity in Society

*It is certainly true that today, when the Church commits herself to works of justice on a human level (and there are few institutions in the world which accomplish what the Catholic Church accomplishes for the poor and disadvantaged), the world praises the Church. But when the Church's work for justice touches on issues and problems which the world no longer sees as bound up with human dignity, like protecting the right to life of every human being from conception to natural death, or when the Church confesses that justice also includes our responsibilities toward God himself, then the world not infrequently reaches for the stones mentioned in our Gospel today.*[1]

—Joseph Cardinal Ratzinger

*Both parties deprecated war, but one of them would make war rather than let the nation survive, and the other would accept war rather than let it perish, and the war came.*[2]

—Abraham Lincoln

The language of battle is interwoven in the history and ongoing struggle for freedom and justice because it is, frankly, an engagement between the forces of good and evil. And if "evil" is too strong a word for this conversation, Saint Augustine perfectly defined its meaning as "the absence of good". There is "not good" in the movement to end human

[1]Joseph Cardinal Ratzinger, "Fortieth Anniversary of *Gaudium et Spes*: Homily of Card. Joseph Ratzinger", Mar. 18, 2005, http://www.vatican.va/roman_curia/congregations/cfaith/documents/rc_con_cfaith_doc_20050318_ratzinger-gaudium-spes_en.html.

[2]Abraham Lincoln, *Second Inaugural Address* (Mar. 4, 1865), *PBS*, http://www.pbs.org/civilwar/war/lincoln_address2.html. Reprinted by permission of the Abraham Lincoln Association.

life at its most vulnerable stages and in denying entire classes of people their rights.

The legacy of the Rev. Dr. Martin Luther King in his unceasing commitment to battling forces against human rights for "all God's children" is the movement he led with a foundation on God's revealed truth about mankind and freedom, and its nonviolent resistance to the tyranny of untruth and injustice. In one of his lesser-known addresses, "Our God Is Marching On!" King addressed a contingent of the civil rights movement that had started "more than eight thousand" strong "on a mighty walk" from Selma, Alabama, to Montgomery, where he said a new philosophy had been born out of their struggle.

"Out of this struggle, more than bus desegregation was won; a new idea, more powerful than guns or clubs was born", he declared. And that civil rights movement "took it and carried it across the South in epic battles that electrified the nation and the world.... And from the wells of this democratic spirit, the nation finally forced Congress to write legislation in the hope that it would eradicate the stain" of racism and segregation.

> Once more the method of nonviolent resistance was unsheathed from its scabbard, and once again an entire community was mobilized to confront the adversary.... If the worst in American life lurked in its dark streets, the best of American instincts arose passionately from across the nation to overcome it. There never was a moment in American history more honorable and more inspiring than the pilgrimage of clergymen and laymen of every race and faith pouring into Selma to face danger at the side of its embattled Negroes [African Americans].
>
> The confrontation of good and evil compressed in the tiny community of Selma generated the massive power to turn the whole nation on a new course.[3]

Dr. King's words convey much the same context and animating spirit of today's civil and spiritual battle over fundamental human rights. In a historical sense, they also converge with the message of "The Battle Hymn of the Republic", which is not only sung at festivities and rallies

[3] Rev. Dr. Martin Luther King, Jr., "Address at the Conclusion of the Selma to Montgomery March: Our God Is Marching On!" (Mar. 25, 1965), The Martin Luther King, Jr., Research and Education Institute, http://mlk-kpp01.stanford.edu/index.php/kingpapers/article/our_god_is_marching_on/, © 1965 Dr. Martin Luther King, Jr., © renewed 1993 Coretta Scott King, reprinted by arrangement with The Heirs to the Estate of Martin Luther King Jr., c/o Writers House as agent for the proprietor New York, N.Y.

and ceremonies marking national holidays, but in churches in honor of those occasions. Why in churches? Because of its message. So similar to King's reference of "nonviolent resistance" being "unsheathed from its scabbard" is "He hath loosed the fateful lightning of His terrible swift sword: His truth is marching on."

"The Battle Hymn of the Republic" was written by Julia Ward Howe in 1861 and became best known as a Civil War song, and later one that inspired American soldiers during World War II, and civil rights activists during the 1960s. Its stanzas speak to all the issues of today's culture wars, actions that proceed from challenges to and defense of natural law based on divine revelation—in other words, between believers in "God-given rights" and those who believe that rights come from no source other than cultural and political consensus.

The words of the hymn can well apply to today's right-to-life movement manifested in the annual March for Life on the Mall of Washington, which has grown to over half a million people. Those crowds, increasingly filled with youth each year, march from a rallying point, where they hear rousing talks and exhortations, to the Supreme Court, where they hope to see the *Roe v. Wade* abortion law overturned. It's a peaceful demonstration, filled with singing and chanting crowds dedicated and determined to defend the dignity of all human life from conception to natural death.

In more recent times, the March for Marriage formed, with an enormous group turning out at the first March for Marriage in Paris on January 13, 2013, before the French legislature enacted law that redefined marriage. A second one was held on April 21, 2013, and another massive March for Marriage was held in Paris on May 26, 2013. In the United States, the first March for Marriage was held on March 26, 2013, in Washington on the day the Supreme Court held hearings on marriage law in the Proposition 8 challenge.

The late Fr. Richard John Neuhaus, a former civil rights activist who marched with Dr. Martin Luther King, Jr., and with pro-lifers at the March for Life, wrote about what inspires and motivates this movement and why it will continue—and how it will continue.

> Ours is a movement of love, and if it ever stops being that, it will cease to claim our commitment. It is a movement of love for God, and of love for the neighbor whom others would exclude from the community of caring and concern.

Seldom in human history have so many done so much for so long out of no rational reason other than the relentless imperative of love. And when you are weary of the struggle—when you're tempted to despair—remember that to us has been given the gift, and with the gift the obligation of sustaining, amidst the darkness, the luminous moment of love that is the pro-life cause.

It has been a long moment, this pro-life struggle, and it will be longer still....

... So long as we have the gift of life, we must protect the gift of life. So long as it is threatened, so long must it be defended. This is the time to brace ourselves for the long term, for we are today laying the foundations for the pro-life movement of the 21st Century. Pray that the foundations are firm, for we have not yet seen fully the fury of the storm that is upon us.

But we have not the right to despair. We do not have the right, and do not have a reason to despair, if, that is, we understand that our entire struggle is premised, not upon a victory to be achieved, but a victory that has been achieved. If we understand that, far from despair, we have right and reason to rejoice that we are called at such a time as this—a time of testing, a time of truth.

The encroaching culture of death shall not prevail, for we know, as we read in St. John's gospel, that "the light shineth in the darkness, and the darkness will not overcome it." The darkness will *never* overcome that light.[4]

## What Must We Do?

Marching orders, so to speak, often come from homilies and addresses drawn from the Gospel for Christian citizens, and these days the clergy up to the highest levels are exhorting the faithful to act on these messages rather than just be inspired by them. Before the cardinals of the world entered the Conclave of 2013 to elect the successor to Pope Benedict XVI, they exchanged concerns and insights about the Church at that moment in time and hopes for its future in the series of Congregations held for that purpose. Individual cardinals gave brief "Interventions", short speeches, to express their views. Cardinal Jorge Bergoglio gave a particularly intriguing one, according to at least two cardinals who talked about it later. Given that the cardinals would go on to elect Bergoglio to the papacy, his remarks merit special attention.

[4] Fr. Richard John Neuhaus, "The Luminous Moment of Love—The Spirit of the Pro-Life Movement", *Life Insight*, 1994; reprinted as "A Pastor's Insight", by Life Issues Institute, no. 39-22 (Apr. 8, 2003), http://www.lifeissues.org/radio/r2003/04/r39-22.htm.

Cardinal Bergoglio's Intervention was his own diagnosis of the problems in the Church, which he saw as pretty much based on the issue of evangelization and the way Christians and even clergy either were or weren't doing that at the time well enough. He said the Church was being too "self-referential", an interesting new concept to some prelates who took it to heart. "Evangelizing pre-supposes a desire in the Church to come out of herself. The Church is called to come out of herself and to go to the peripheries, not only geographically, but also the existential peripheries: the mystery of sin, of pain, of injustice, of ignorance and indifference to religion, of intellectual currents, and of all misery."[5]

Those concerned with building a free, just, and humane society can't keep the light to which Richard John Neuhaus referred under a bushel basket, to continue his biblical reference and recall what Jesus Christ taught his disciples before sending them out to change the culture (Mt 5:15). Pope Francis put particular emphasis on the Christian witness from the beginning of his papacy, something for which, prior to that, his ministry had been known.

Picking up on the thought at the end of the last chapter, we have the ability through modern social communications to reach the whole world, to go around gatekeeper media and spread messages. We were told to do that in the Second Vatican Council's document *Inter Mirifica*, Pope John Paul II's message in his 2005 Apostolic Letter *Rapid Development*, and successive messages from Pope Benedict on World Day of Communications, among countless other opportunities he took to exhort the faithful to engage social media and humanize it and give people hope.

As Archbishop Chaput said in his book *Render Unto Caesar*, "Catholics who know their faith also know that publicly opposing racism and publicly opposing abortion flow from the same Catholic beliefs about the dignity of the human person. Both evils are inexcusably wrong. On matters like these, the church has the duty to teach the world—not the reverse."[6]

But he also makes the point that "many American Catholics tend to forget the role the church has played throughout history in shaping the

[5] "Bergoglio's Intervention: A Diagnosis of the Problems in the Church", Vatican Radio, Mar. 27, 2013, http://en.radiovaticana.va/news/2013/03/27/bergoglios_intervention:_a_diagnosis_of_the_problems_in_the_church/en1-677269.

[6] Charles J. Chaput, *Render Unto Caesar: Serving the Nation by Living Our Catholic Beliefs in Political Life* (New York: Doubleday Religion, 2008), p. 59.

public square. Due to that ignorance, they often accept a bad version of their own story.... If we accept a narrative of our own story written by skeptics of the Christian faith, we are not being 'open' or balanced. We are colluding in a lie."[7]

He was talking mostly in that paragraph about celebrity atheists on the best-seller list, who keep turning out books rewriting our history or distorting our beliefs as Catholics and other Christians. But a smaller though more widespread version of that is happening every day in news stories put out by media who changed their style manuals to call pro-life people "anti-abortion", "abortion opponents", "opponents of women's rights", "reproductive rights opponents", "marriage equality opponents", etc. Christians must not be defined by what they oppose but by what they propose and uphold.

Here's a great example. In May 2013, an article appeared in *Christianity Today* titled "My Train Wreck Conversion". It was an exquisite example and witness of how to reach people as the former Cardinal Bergoglio urged by going "to the peripheries, existential peripheries", to "the mystery of indifference to religion, of intellectual currents", and all the rest. The article's intriguing subhead was "As a leftist lesbian professor, I despised Christians. Then I somehow became one." How could you not be drawn in by that?

> As a university professor, I tired of students who seemed to believe that "knowing Jesus" meant knowing little else. Christians in particular were bad readers, always seizing opportunities to insert a Bible verse into a conversation with the same point as a punctuation mark: to end it rather than deepen it.
>
> Stupid. Pointless. Menacing. That's what I thought of Christians and their god Jesus ...
>
> As a professor of English and women's studies, on the track to becoming a tenured radical, I cared about morality, justice, and compassion. Fervent for the worldviews of Freud, Hegel, Marx, and Darwin, I strove to stand with the disempowered. I valued morality. And I probably could have stomached Jesus and his band of warriors if it weren't for how other cultural forces buttressed the Christian Right. Pat Robertson's quip from the 1992 Republican National Convention pushed me over the edge: "Feminism," he sneered, "encourages women to leave their husbands,

[7] Ibid., pp. 58–59.

> kill their children, practice witchcraft, destroy capitalism, and become lesbians." Indeed. The surround sound of Christian dogma comingling with Republican politics demanded my attention.[8]

She makes compelling points while explaining how happy she was at the time publishing her tenure book and being "a leftist lesbian professor" advancing her post through allegiances that fit her worldview.

> My partner and I shared many vital interests: aids activism, children's health and literacy, Golden Retriever rescue, our Unitarian Universalist church, to name a few. Even if you believed the ghost stories promulgated by Robertson and his ilk, it was hard to argue that my partner and I were anything but good citizens and caregivers. The GLBT community values hospitality and applies it with skill, sacrifice, and integrity.
>
> I began researching the Religious Right and their politics of hatred against queers like me. To do this, I would need to read the one book that had, in my estimation, gotten so many people off track: the Bible. While on the lookout for some Bible scholar to aid me in my research, I launched my first attack on the unholy trinity of Jesus, Republican politics, and patriarchy, in the form of an article in the local newspaper about Promise Keepers. It was 1997.[9]

Give credit where it's due, and she deserves plenty for being proactive in researching ideas and politics and religion that ran counter to her beliefs, better to understand and engage them. That is the intellectual tradition of Thomas Aquinas. She applied Thomistic critical-thinking skills, and she was open to where they lead (in spite of her preconceived notion of—and distaste for—where that was).

Her article drew a lot of response ranging from "hate mail" to "fan mail", but there was one that threw her off base.

> It was from the pastor of the Syracuse Reformed Presbyterian Church. It was a kind and inquiring letter. Ken Smith encouraged me to explore the kind of questions I admire: How did you arrive at your interpretations? How do you know you are right? Do you believe in God? Ken didn't argue with my article; rather, he asked me to defend the presuppositions that undergirded it. I didn't know how to respond to it, so I threw it away.

[8] Rosaria Champagne Butterfield, "My Train Wreck Conversion", *Christianity Today*, Jan./Feb. 2013, p. 1, http://www.christianitytoday.com/ct/2013/january-february/my-train-wreck-conversion.html?visit_source=facebook&start=1.

[9] Ibid.

> Later that night, I fished it out of the recycling bin and put it back on my desk, where it stared at me for a week, confronting me with the worldview divide that demanded a response. As a postmodern intellectual, I operated from a historical materialist worldview, but Christianity is a supernatural worldview. Ken's letter punctured the integrity of my research project without him knowing it.[10]

The account is a remarkable witness to intellectual honesty, to pursuing clarity with charity, to changing hearts and minds one at a time if necessary, respecting human dignity and engaging everyone as already having it, equally and inherently, no matter who they are or what they believe.

> I continued reading the Bible, all the while fighting the idea that it was inspired. But the Bible got to be bigger inside me than I. It overflowed into my world. I fought against it with all my might....
>
> I was a thinker. I was paid to read books and write about them. I expected that in all areas of life, understanding came *before* obedience. And I wanted God to show me, on my terms, why homosexuality was a sin. I wanted to be the judge, not one being judged.
>
> But the verse promised understanding after obedience. I wrestled with the question: Did I really want to understand homosexuality from God's point of view, or did I just want to argue with him? I prayed that night that God would give me the willingness to obey before I understood.[11]

The prayer was answered.

> Then, one ordinary day, I came to Jesus, openhanded and naked. In this war of worldviews, Ken was there. [His wife] Floy was there. The church that had been praying for me for years was there. Jesus triumphed. And I was a broken mess. Conversion was a train wreck. I did not want to lose everything that I loved. But the voice of God sang a sanguine love song in the rubble of my world. I weakly believed that if Jesus could conquer death, he could make right my world. I drank, tentatively at first, then passionately, of the solace of the Holy Spirit. I rested in private peace, then community, and today in the shelter of a covenant family, where one calls me "wife" and many call me "mother."[12]

[10] Ibid.

[11] Ibid., p. 2, http://www.christianitytoday.com/ct/2013/january-february/my-train-wreck-conversion.html?visit_source=facebook&start=2.

[12] Ibid., p. 3, http://www.christianitytoday.com/ct/2013/january-february/my-train-wreck-conversion.html?visit_source=facebook&start=3.

This is an amazing story, personally told and profoundly offered as a testimony. It relates to homosexuality, marriage, religion, politics, and academia—basically, the culture war today. This war has to be engaged through the power of personal witness and the truth of the message.

Barbara Nicolosi, founder of the Act One Program, a nonprofit group that trains and mentors Christians for careers as Hollywood writers and executives, also teaches students the entertainment arts and especially the nearly lost art of storytelling. She frequently and passionately makes the argument that we're losing the culture to slickly produced and highly marketed movies that promote "the culture of death" and, especially these days, euthanasia. In her article "Exposing Euthanasia through the Arts", Nicolosi calls out Christians to see the signs of the times and act on them.

> The evidence is undeniable: Somewhere in the middle of the Terri Schiavo tragedy, Hollywood and the cultural left climbed aboard the latest human-killing bandwagon and have since thrown the weight of their talent and creativity behind it. As with abortion, the forces of darkness are outmaneuvering the forces of good on what will certainly be the moral issue of the 21st century.
>
> If we lose the fight on euthanasia, we lose our souls. By removing suffering and the meaning of suffering from our culture, we make the final step in denying and defying our creature-hood....
>
> Our response to the mercy-killing machine must be more than an occasional op-ed piece; we need a shrewd and all-encompassing cultural strategy if we are going to make a good fight in the euthanasia war.
>
> Shrewd means that we fight smart. It means appealing to the emotions of the masses through stories, not non-fiction tomes.... Heroes, not pundits.[13]

Nonfiction tomes have their place, too. But she's making a very important point here, and we'd better get it.

There is and always has been power in story and storytelling, images and impressions. People react on emotion before intellect. Christians have to become better at reaching people through the power of the word and the art of storytelling.

That's an argument the Breakpoint Christian media dynamos have been making these days. Eric Metaxas, best-selling author of *Bonhoeffer:*

[13] Barbara Nicolosi, "Exposing Euthanasia through the Arts", *Crisis Magazine*, June 3, 2011, http://www.crisismagazine.com/2011/exposing-euthanasia-through-the-arts.

*Pastor, Prophet, Martyr, Spy* and *Amazing Grace: William Wilberforce and the Heroic Campaign to End Slavery*, is all over the media engaging cultural issues and Christian faith. In his column "Not Sermons but Stories", Metaxas says we need to change the way we interact with the culture. "The vast majority of the stories that permeate our culture are told by people whose worldview is diametrically opposed to ours."[14] Metaxas continues:

> Christians produced great art and culture for centuries, and we can do it again. But there are no shortcuts. The church needs to teach its members a strong and consistent Christian worldview, and then support and encourage those with artistic gifts to pursue their calling....
>
> Re-shaping the culture is a noble goal. But our first goal should be to be so soaked in the Christian faith and worldview that the stories we tell—and the lives we live—will naturally speak of the beauty, and goodness and love of Christ.[15]

Metaxas' Breakpoint colleague, John Stonestreet, challenges that idea further, and he makes a compelling point here about something he discovered from reading Neil Postman's book *Amusing Ourselves to Death*.

> In it, [Neil Postman] contrasts the futurist visions in George Orwell's "1984" and Aldous Huxley's "Brave New World."
>
> At first glance their visions were similar; but Postman suggests otherwise. "What Orwell feared," Postman wrote, "were those who would ban books. What Huxley feared was that there would be no reason to ban a book, because there would be no one who wanted to read one.... Orwell feared that the truth would be concealed from us. Huxley feared the truth would be drowned in a sea of irrelevance. Orwell feared we would become a captive culture. Huxley feared we would become a trivial culture.[16]

Where are we today in these prophetic visions? Which most closely resembles our culture? Are we even able to discern the truth, and does it still resonate?

[14] Eric Metaxas, "Not Sermons but Stories: Engaging in Culture the Right Way", *Breakpoint*, Jan. 8, 2013, http://www.breakpoint.org/bpcommentaries/entry/13/21183.

[15] Ibid.

[16] John Stonestreet, "Raising Eric Metaxas: Challenging Consumers of Culture", *Breakpoint*, Jan. 10, 2013, http://www.breakpoint.org/bpcommentaries/entry/13/21160?utm_source=feedburner&utm_medium=feed&utm_campaign=Feed%3A+BpCommentaries+%28BreakPoint+Commentaries%29.

## A Strong Witness

Cardinal Francis George is one of the American bishops regularly challenging the culture and politics and the threats they pose to human dignity. His column in the *Catholic New World* just before the November 2012 election was titled "The Wrong Side of History". In it, he picks up on a theme Pope Benedict often addressed, because it remains so prevalent and timely.

> Communism imposed a total way of life based upon the belief that God does not exist. Secularism is communism's better-scrubbed bedfellow. A small irony of history cropped up at the United Nations ... when Russia joined the majority of other nations to defeat the United States and the western European nations that wanted to declare that killing the unborn should be a universal human right. Who is on the wrong side of history now?
>
> The [2012] political campaign has brought to the surface of our public life the anti-religious sentiment, much of it explicitly anti-Catholic, that has been growing in this country for several decades. The secularizing of our culture is a much larger issue than political causes or the outcome of the current electoral campaign, important though that is.[17]

Here he repeats a story that has sort of become part of the Chicago Catholic lore.

> Speaking a few years ago to a group of priests, entirely outside of the current political debate, I was trying to express in overly dramatic fashion what the complete secularization of our society could bring. I was responding to a question and I never wrote down what I said, but the words were captured on somebody's smart phone and have now gone viral on Wikipedia and elsewhere in the electronic communications world. I am (correctly) quoted as saying that I expected to die in bed, my successor will die in prison and his successor will die a martyr in the public square. What is omitted from the reports is a final phrase I added about the bishop who follows a possibly martyred bishop: "His successor will pick up the shards of a ruined society and slowly help rebuild civilization, as the church has done so often in human history." What I said is not "prophetic" but a way to force people to think outside of the usual categories that limit and sometimes poison both private and public discourse.[18]

[17] Francis Cardinal George, O.M.I., "The Wrong Side of History", *Catholic New World* , Oct. 21–Nov. 3, 2012, http://www.catholicnewworld.com/cnwonline/2012/1021/cardinal.aspx.

[18] Ibid.

That is a very instructive point.

> An earlier Archbishop of Chicago once tried his hand at reading the signs of his times.... Cardinal Mundelein spoke of how the public protests of the bishops had been silenced in the German media, leaving the church in Germany more "helpless" than it had ever been.
>
> He then added: "There is no guarantee that the battle-front may not stretch someday into our own land. *Hodie mihi cras tibi.* (Today it's me; tomorrow, you). If we show no interest in this matter now, if we shrug our shoulders and mutter ... it is not our fight, if we don't back up the Holy Father when we have a chance, well, when our turn comes, we too will be fighting alone."[19]

That recalls the message two great Evangelical leaders issued in an open letter to their church members after the HHS mandate was issued and Catholic bishops were leading the battle and campaign to defend religious liberty and conscience rights in America. It appeared in *Christianity Today*, entitled "First They Came for the Catholics: Obama's Contraceptive Mandate". Its authors were Dr. Timothy George and the late Chuck Colson.

> The Catholic bishops in America have responded quickly, decrying the Administration's decision for what it is—an egregious, dangerous violation of religious liberty—and mobilizing a vast grassroots movement to persuade the Administration to reverse its decision.
>
> We evangelicals must stand unequivocally with our Roman Catholic brothers and sisters. Because when the government violates the religious liberty of one group, it threatens the religious liberty of all....
>
> Three years ago, when we co-authored the Manhattan Declaration, we predicted that the time would come when Christians would have to face the very real prospect of civil disobedience—that we would have to choose sides: God or Caesar.
>
> Certainly for the Catholics and for many of us evangelicals, that time is already upon us.
>
> We would urge you, therefore, to raise your voice against this unjust mandate that violates our first freedom as Americans.[20]

They asked people to take an active civic role in contacting their elected representatives and asking them to protect religious liberty and

[19] Ibid.

[20] Timothy George and Chuck Colson, "First They Came for the Catholics: Obama's Contraceptive Mandate", *Christianity Today*, Feb. 8, 2012, http://www.christianitytoday.com/ct/2012/februaryweb-only/catholics-contraceptive-mandate.html.

conscience rights. They also asked them to participate in the *Manhattan Declaration* movement. And then they asked people to pray for the nation's leaders.

> We do not exaggerate when we say that this is the greatest threat to religious freedom in our lifetime. We cannot help but think of the words attributed to German pastor Martin Niemoeller, reflecting on the Nazi terror:
>
> First they came for the Socialists, and I
> did not speak out—
> Because I was not a Socialist.
>
> Then they came for the Trade Unionists,
> and I did not speak out—
> Because I was not a Trade Unionist.
>
> Then they came for the Jews, and I did
> not speak out—Because I was not a Jew.
>
> Then they came for me—and there was
> no one left to speak for me.[21]

Catholics not traditionally comfortable with speaking out on the hot-button social issues of the day learned quickly when their right to express their beliefs publicly and order their lives and businesses accordingly was threatened by the government for the first real time.

## "Onward"

There is no turning back, now that Church leaders and faithful are so engaged in public policy and having to defend rights we used to take for granted. Dr. Martin Luther King's rousing talk, "Our God Is Marching On!" encourages that engagement with a timeless message.

> Let us march on ballot boxes until we send to our city councils, state legislatures, and the United States Congress, men who will not fear to do justly, love mercy, and walk humbly with thy God.
>
> Let us march on ballot boxes until brotherhood becomes more than a meaningless word in an opening prayer, but the order of the day on every legislative agenda.

[21] Ibid.

> Let us march on ballot boxes until all ... God's children will be able to walk the earth in decency and honor....
>
> The road ahead is not altogether a smooth one. There are no broad highways that lead us easily and inevitably to quick solutions. But we must keep going....
>
> The only normalcy that we will settle for is the normalcy that recognizes the dignity and worth of all of God's children.... The only normalcy that we will settle for is the normalcy of brotherhood, the normalcy of true peace, the normalcy of justice.[22]

We cannot entrust that to leaders of nations, working through diplomatic channels or top-level meetings, said Pope John XXIII in *Pacem in Terris*, because they are no longer able to solve world problems, achieve peace, or assure justice.

> The world will never be the dwelling place of peace, till peace has found a home in the heart of each and every man, till every man preserves in himself the order ordained by God to be preserved. That is why St. Augustine asks the question: "Does your mind desire the strength to gain the mastery over your passions? Let it submit to a greater power, and it will conquer all beneath it. And peace will be in you—true, sure, most ordered peace."[23]

A homily Pope Francis gave early in his papacy perfectly carries on that message, with an interesting emphasis on the concept of "submitting to conquer".

> Christians are called to do the great work of evangelizing to the ends of the world in a spirit of humility rather than an attitude of conquering, Pope Francis said....
>
> "But she does not go forth alone: she goes forth with Jesus ... the Lord works with all those who preach the Gospel. This is the magnanimity that Christians should have."
>
> A timid, or "pusillanimous" Christian, he added, "is incomprehensible: this magnanimity is part of the Christian vocation: always more and more, more and more, more and more, always onwards."[24]

[22] King, "Our God Is Marching On!", http://mlk-kpp01.stanford.edu/index.php/kingpapers/article/our_god_is_marching_on/, © 1965 Dr. Martin Luther King, Jr., © renewed 1993 Coretta Scott King, reprinted by arrangement with The Heirs to the Estate of Martin Luther King Jr., c/o Writers House as agent for the proprietor New York, N.Y.

[23] Pope John XXIII, *Pacem in Terris* (Apr. 11, 1963), no. 165.

[24] "Church Must Evangelize Humbly, Pope Francis Reflects", *Catholic News Agency*, Apr. 25, 2013, http://www.catholicnewsagency.com/news/church-must-evangelize-humbly-pope-francis-reflects.

Shortly before the 2012 presidential election, a "Leadership Summit" was held in a private remote headquarters just outside Chicago, with close to a dozen well-known or influential speakers from different parts of the country and both political parties on the topic of religious liberty in America. The gathering included a congressman, a state attorney general, a former prisoner of war, members of local, national, and international media, a rabbi, a priest, and a Muslim woman attorney, along with corporate leaders and heads of faith-based charitable organizations.

The master of ceremonies shared an anecdotal story about a visit to places around the historic battles of Concord and Lexington, including the Minuteman Museum near Concord, Massachusetts. Sitting in a darkened auditorium, she watched and heard a presentation of the historic ride of Paul Revere, one that took place across the surrounding roads and countryside of that auditorium. She said the story and visual account of the events of that night were deeply stirring, when Revere took news to his countrymen of approaching forces that threatened their freedom. The trail he rode was shown overhead and lit up in red, one light at a time, as the narrator recounted the details.

Soon the single lights representing small towns and villages started spreading quickly into a scattering of lights beyond the town as people spread the word fast and, exponentially, sounded the alert and roused the response from so many citizens that they were able to prepare a resistance force and hold their ground. All this happened because they had prepared, together, as the threat had progressed earlier on, and because Paul Revere took the action he could to raise his voice for the defense of liberty.

It was a profound example of what one person can do when he takes whatever action he can and uses his voice to speak out wherever he can.

Rev. Dr. Martin Luther King, Jr., did that in marches with thousands of civil rights activists. Others do that in marches that continue today. Paul Revere did it on horseback. They did it for the cause of liberty and justice for all.

[25] Abraham Lincoln, "Speech at Chicago, Illinois (July 10, 1858)", in Abraham Lincoln Association, *The Collected Works of Abraham Lincoln*, ed. Roy P. Basler, vol. 2 (New Brunswick, N.J.; Rutgers University Press, 1953), p. 502. Reprinted by permission of the Abraham Lincoln Association.

The cause and call endure.

*I leave you, hoping that the lamp of liberty will burn in your bosoms until there shall no longer be a doubt that all men are created free and equal.*[25]

—Abraham Lincoln

## Let's Be Clear:

1. **Our actions are crucially important.** Actions express our inner world of thought and have immense power to influence others. The public square is where our personal selves are expressed and come into contact with others. Pope Paul VI noted: "Modern man listens more willingly to witnesses than to teachers, and if he does listen to teachers, it is because they are witnesses."[26]
2. **We are called to fight for a just society for all.** Archbishop Charles Chaput instructs: "Catholics who know their faith also know that publicly opposing racism and publicly opposing abortion flow from the same Catholic beliefs about the dignity of the human person. Both evils are inexcusably wrong. On matters like these, the church has the duty to teach the world—not the reverse."[27] This is true not just personally in the realm of our convictions, but also *publicly* in the realm of our actions and in civic society (i.e., as Jesus did).
3. **We must fight to uphold the non-negotiables!** These are not matters of personal conviction or opinion. We cannot have a true, just, and virtuous society without them.

> Worship pleasing to God can never be a purely private matter, without consequences for our relationships with others: it demands a public witness to our faith. Evidently, this is true for all the baptized, yet it is especially incumbent upon those who, by virtue of their social or political position, must make decisions regarding fundamental values, such as respect for human life, its defence from conception to natural death, the family built upon marriage between a man and a woman, the freedom to educate one's children and the promotion of the common good in all its forms. These values are not negotiable.[28]

[26] Pope Paul VI, *Evangelii Nuntiandi* (1975), no. 41.

[27] Chaput, *Render Unto Caesar*, p. 59.

[28] Pope Benedict XVI, *Sacramentum Caritatis* (2007), no. 83, http://www.vatican.va/holy_father/benedict_xvi/apost_exhortations/documents/hf_ben-xvi_exh_20070222_sacramentum-caritatis_en.html.

# FURTHER READING

## Chapter 1:

- *Manhattan Declaration: A Call of Christian Conscience* (Nov. 20, 2009), http://manhattandeclaration.org.
- United States Conference of Catholic Bishops, *Forming Consciences for Faithful Citizenship: A Call to Political Responsibility from the Catholic Bishops of the United States* (Nov. 2007), http://www.usccb.org/issues-and-action/faithful-citizenship/forming-consciences-for-faithful-citizenship-part-one.cfm.
- Rev. Dr. Martin Luther King, Jr., Letter from Birmingham Jail, Apr. 16, 1963; African Studies Center, University of Pennsylvania, http://www.africa.upenn.edu/Articles_Gen/Letter_Birmingham.html.
- United States Conference of Catholic Bishops, *Living the Gospel of Life: A Challenge to American Catholics* (1998), http://www.usccb.org/issues-and-action/human-life-and-dignity/abortion/living-the-gospel-of-life.cfm.

## Chapter 2:

- Congregation for the Doctrine of the Faith, *Declaration on Procured Abortion* (Nov. 18, 1974), http://www.vatican.va/roman_curia/congregations/cfaith/documents/rc_con_cfaith_doc_19741118_declaration-abortion_en.html.
- Congregation for the Doctrine of the Faith, "Instruction on Respect for Human Life in Its Origin and on the Dignity of Procreation: Replies to Certain Questions of the Day: *Donum Vitae*" (Feb. 22, 1987), http://www.vatican.va/roman_curia/congregations/cfaith/documents/rc_con_cfaith_doc_19870222_respect-for-human-life_en.html.
- Pope John Paul II, *Evangelium Vitae* (Mar. 25, 1995), http://www.vatican.va/holy_father/john_paul_ii/encyclicals/documents/hf_jp-ii_enc_25031995_evangelium-vitae_en.html.

## Chapter 3:

- Pope John Paul II, "Address of John Paul II to the Participants in the International Congress on 'Life-Sustaining Treatments and Vegetative State: Scientific Advances and Ethical Dilemmas'" (Mar. 20, 2004), http://www.vatican.va/holy_father/john_paul_ii/speeches/2004/march/documents/hf_jp-ii_spe_20040320_congress-fiamc_en.html.
- Congregation for the Doctrine of the Faith, "Responses to Certain Questions of the United States Conference of Catholic Bishops Concerning Artificial Nutrition and Hydration" (Aug. 1, 2007), http://www.vatican.va/roman_curia/congregations/cfaith/documents/rc_con_cfaith_doc_20070801_risposte-usa_en.html.
- Congregation for the Doctrine of the Faith, *Declaration on Euthanasia* (May 5, 1980), http://www.vatican.va/roman_curia/congregations/cfaith/documents/rc_con_cfaith_doc_19800505_euthanasia_en.html.
- United States Conference of Catholic Bishops, *Ethical and Religious Directives for Catholic Health Facilities* (Nov. 17, 2009), http://www.usccb.org/issues-and-action/human-life-and-dignity/health-care/upload/Ethical-Religious-Directives-Catholic-Health-Care-Services-fifth-edition-2009.pdf.

## Chapter 4:

- Congregation for the Doctrine of the Faith, "Letter to the Bishops of the Catholic Church on the Pastoral Care of Homosexual Persons" (Oct. 1, 1986), http://www.vatican.va/roman_curia/congregations/cfaith/documents/rc_con_cfaith_doc_19861001_homosexual-persons_en.html.
- United States Conference of Catholic Bishops, "Frequently Asked Questions about the Defense of Marriage" (Nov. 14, 2006), http://www.usccb.org/issues-and-action/marriage-and-family/marriage/promotion-and-defense-of-marriage/frequently-asked-questions-on-defense-of-marriage.cfm#m4.

## Chapter 5:

- Second Vatican Council, *Dignitatis Humanae* (Dec. 7, 1965), http://www.vatican.va/archive/hist_councils/ii_vatican_council/documents/vat-ii_decl_19651207_dignitatis-humanae_en.html.

- United States Conference of Catholic Bishops, *Our First, Most Cherished Liberty* (Apr. 12, 2012), http://www.usccb.org/issues-and-action/religious-liberty/our-first-most-cherished-liberty.cfm.

## Chapter 6:

- Pope John XXIII, *Pacem in Terris* (Apr. 11, 1963), http://www.vatican.va/holy_father/john_xxiii/encyclicals/documents/hf_j-xxiii_enc_11041963_pacem_en.html.